Solutional Politics:

How one person CAN make a difference

By Todd Haffner

Contents

0 Thanksgiving

Thanksgiving 2002. The extended family is gathering at our house. I'm looking forward to a day with the family, a day of relaxing, watching football, listening to grandpa snoring, giving thanks for life, and having lots and lots of turkey.

Some of us are sitting at the kitchen table. My school teacher aunt looks directly at me and says, "Why is Bush invading Iraq? I can't believe he wants to do that."

Why she is bringing this up, I don't know. I thought everyone knew that you don't discuss politics or religion at family gatherings. But I try to be helpful. "He claims it's because they have weapons of mass destruction. He's afraid they could do more harm to us than what happened on 9/11."

She's determined. "We shouldn't be going into another war."

"Well, the Democrats are supporting him."

"It's only because they have to." She pauses; I can see she's growing more irritated. "Look at all the money he's spending."

I calmly state that "It's congress that controls the spending, not the President. It's not all on the President; he's just part of the process."

"He's giving tax breaks to the rich. He doesn't care about the budget. He should be giving more money to help the poor."

"I agree, somewhat. I think he should care about the budget. I'm annoyed that he's not trying to balance the budget."

"I can't believe he wants to start another war. What is wrong with him?   Why   are   you   supporting   him?"

"I'm not a Republican."

"You vote for them."

"Sometimes, yes. Sometimes I vote for Democrats. You can't just blame the Republicans; the Democrats are just as guilty."

"How can you say that? Clinton had a balanced budget, and then Bush came along and screwed it all up."

It's at this point that my Republican father-in-law, who is a Korean War veteran, decides to chime in. "The Democrats are nothing but a bunch of gays and Communists. They should all be shot."

"Don't say that. Why would you say that?" I know he's being facetious, but I'm afraid things could get worse.

My aunt glares at him and scowls. "And I suppose you want to go to war, too?"

Uh oh, I'm really nervous.

My father-in-law then says, "I think we should just nuke them all."

Yes, he said it. Pandemonium. Lightning, tornadoes, volcanic eruptions, earthquakes. I stay quiet as their voices get louder; after a minute, I decide to slip away from the kitchen table.

I can hear my father-in-law cursing and my aunt trying to talk over him as I head into the kitchen to check on the turkey. Before I know it, my wife is next to me.

The quiet anger in her voice is something husbands dread. "Look what you started."

"I didn't start anything."

"Yes, you did! Listen to them."

"I didn't do anything. Your aunt started making political statements, and all I did was state some facts and ask some questions."

Her whispers are now dripping with venom. "Yes, and you shouldn't have done that! You should have just kept your mouth shut!"

"But I even partially agreed with her."

"You shouldn't have said anything!"

"I'm going outside." I need to cool off. The cold air feels good as I escape to the garage. I can't figure out what the heck just happened.

A few minutes pass. I'm still fuming. The door opens. I notice it's quiet in the house. My sister-in-law joins me in the garage. She says, "I think you better go back in. I think your wife is going to kill your aunt and your father-in-law."

Well, at least she isn't going to kill me. I feel a little relief. "What do you mean my father-in-law? He's your father."

"Not when he's like this. He's your father-in-law. I disown him."

"So, why is she so upset? What happened?"

"Your father-in-law just kept antagonizing your aunt. He just kept disagreeing with everything she said while cussing and swearing even more."

"So? What else is new? He can be that way sometimes."

"Your aunt, who doesn't have any kids of her own, just told your wife that you are both bad parents and that she can't believe that you are allowed to raise children."

"What? Because of a political discussion we aren't fit to raise children?"

"I'm just telling you, you need to go inside to your wife."

I go back in and see my wife standing in the living room, surrounded by other female family members. Smoke is coming from her ears, literally. I always thought it was just a saying, but there it is.

I walk over to her. I know she's mad, but at least it's not directed at me. I give her a hug. She says, "I'm going to kill my dad."

I hold her and say, "I understand."

Then, while looking out the window at our aunt, who's crying as she's getting into her car to leave, she says, "I don't want her in this house again."

I quietly say, "I agree."

I go into the kitchen to pull out the turkey; it should be done. I can feel the tension emanating from everyone. Happy Freaking Thanksgiving!

1 Reasons

I'm a Director of Information Technology (IT). The license plate on my car reads "ITNERD 1," which brings smiles to people's faces. I'm the typical IT person who works in a business. The other employees know that I'm passionate about computers, that I'm a little quirky, and that I use Garanimals to dress myself. Everyone in the business knows that what IT people do is vital to the business and that the business couldn't run without IT people. Yet, they don't really understand what it is that we do.

I'm also a typical political hobbyist who watches political TV shows, listens to talk radio, votes, and participates in online political forums. I have screamed at the TV and the radio. I tried being nice and politely questioning people's statements on Democratic and Republican political forums; the forums banned me. I don't adhere to their ideology.

I'm an Independent. I consider myself fiscally conservative and socially liberal. Since most ballots have only a Democrat or Republican on them, I hold my nose as I vote for the candidate whom I consider to be the lesser of two evils. I would vote for "none of the above" about 90% of the time, if it were an option.

As an IT person, I bring value to the business when I help other employees be more productive and efficient. I have a foundation of knowledge that I draw upon as I utilize a wide array of skills to accomplish this, knowledge and skills that I wish applied to politics.

Data vs. Information

Data is a single fact, or a few snippets of facts. I have discovered that all the government, non-profit organizations, and international sources for the same data points don't match. Many times, they can differ by as much as 100%. Even departments within the U.S. government don't agree on the same data. As an IT person, inaccurate data is frustrating.

According to the U.S. Department of Commerce, Bureau of Economic Analysis, the per capita income for 2012 was $42,693. According to the Social Security Administration, the national average wage was $44,321.67. So which data point is accurate? Why don't the data points match? Accurate data is important, but there are times when information is more important.

Information is data with context, the accumulation of multiple data points, and the transfer of knowledge. Information helps people determine what is important and what isn't.

For example, if I were to find a piece of paper with numbers on it, I might not think it's important. What are the numbers? What do they represent? Are there more numbers near it? If there are 16 digits, that's more data. If the number is broken into four sections of four numbers, that's more data. Combining the data points and putting them into context implies that the number could be a credit card number. Numbers written on a piece of paper are data. A credit card number written on a piece of paper is information.

The media, politicians, political pundits, and pretty much everybody else who discusses politics only talk about data, not information. They argue over how exact data is. As an IT person, I understand the difference between the two, and I know when one is relevant and important and the other is not, and when both are.

Trends Analysis

Trends analysis is another way to understand the difference between data and information. Trends analysis relies upon information, not data. Not all data and information might be accurate because of how disorganized government reporting is. However, with trends analysis, as long as the information is accurate enough and comes from the same source over a long period of time, the trend becomes what is important.

Finding a piece of paper with a credit card number on it could be an indicator of a bigger problem. As an IT person, I have to check if this is a single occurrence or if there are more credit card numbers written elsewhere. If it's a single occurrence, it could be an anomaly. Multiple occurrences indicate a trend, and that is a big problem.

The Social Security Administration shows the information that the national average wage in 2000 was roughly $32,000, and in 2012 it was roughly $44,000. The U.S. Department of Commerce, Bureau of Economic Analysis, shows the per capita income for 2000 as roughly $30,000 and in 2012 as roughly $43,000. The 12-year trends analysis shows that middle income wages are rising at a rate of roughly three percent a year. That makes the three percent annual pay increases extremely valuable information (and very depressing).

Trends analysis doesn't just look at a single trend, but combines two or more to obtain a larger picture that involves many facets. For instance, in looking at the government spending trend over the last 30 years, and that it has increased by more than six percent a year in addition to the trends in annual per capita income, we gain new information and new insight. If average incomes increase by three percent annually, while government spending increases by six percent annually, the country is in financial trouble.

Communication

Communication is the ability to exchange understanding between two or more people. The people don't have to agree with what is communicated, they just have to understand what is being communicated. In communication, there is a sender and a receiver. The roles of sender and receiver switch back and forth until there is a mutual agreement on the level of understanding.

As an IT person, I have to communicate complex ideas and ensure the receiver understands the nuances or basis of an idea. I sometimes have to communicate why a computer isn't working, why we need to replace a server, why a report isn't accurate, what the limitations of some software are, and many other IT concepts that do a good job of boring people.

If I were to tell management that a single sales person was writing credit card numbers on paper, I'm not communicating. It's my responsibility to ensure the receiver understands the entire message I'm trying to send. It's extremely important I get feed-back from the receiver to ensure the message is clearly understood. I have to provide details, understanding, and explanations.

I explain to management that a salesperson was discovered writing down credit card numbers on paper, but none of the other salespeople do this. I explain that this a security breach and it may also be a minor Payment Card Industry (PCI) compliance issue. I explain that PCI compliance is a set of security standards and rules set by the credit card companies ensuring the safety of credit card information. I explain that the person was retrained and will no longer write down credit card numbers. I have communicated to management the entirety of my message and understanding.

Management's feedback is the other part of communication. They might understand what I said, but the picture in their minds of what the problem was or what the solution was could be different from mine. Management may ask IT how the credit card number is stored on the computer system. They may also ask what the computer system does with the PIN and the expiration date. Management just communicated that IT has more work to do.

Democrats and Republicans don't try to communicate. They don't try to understand each other. They don't ask for feedback and understanding from the opposing party. They are more interested in what they say instead of being interested in what other people say.

Logic

According to the Merriam-Webster Dictionary, logic is:

"A science that deals with the principles and criteria of validity of inference and demonstration."

In normal terminology, that means using facts, true facts, and all the facts when looking at any given situation. Ensure the validity of the facts and ensure these facts are turned into information. Then, utilize the information to decide on the validity of an idea or statement. If there is a disconnect with the facts, then the idea or argument becomes illogical.

If IT were to determine that the credit card number is encrypted when it's entered into the computer system, this is a good thing. However, this leaves a disconnect in the facts and the process. The credit card number has to travel from the customer's computer, through the internet, through our network, and to our database server, where the credit card information is encrypted and stored. The logical question then becomes, what security is in place to protect the credit card number as it travels from the customer's computer to our database server?

The government poverty level for a family of four in 2012 was $23,050. The government also reports that the cost of living varies widely from state to state. There is a disconnect with these facts. How can the government create a single poverty level when the cost of living varies by each state? If one state's cost of living is twice that of another state, then logically, the poverty level for the other state should be twice as high as the first state.

Another disconnect in the data is that the government doesn't state whether the $23,050 is gross income or net income. Net income is gross wages minus taxes, insurance, Social Security, Medicare, and many other possible deductions that can be taken out of a paycheck. Net income is the amount of money people actually receive. The difference between gross income and net income can sometimes be as much as 30 percent. Logically, this means that if the $23,050 is net income, then the gross income poverty level is $32,900.

Logic is one of the greatest skills an IT person has. Some of my biggest frustrations with politicians and the government stem from their sheer lack of logic.

Root Cause Analysis

Root cause analysis is a quality control process that's used to get to the root or core of a problem. It's a process that helps ensure that solutions don't just fix symptoms. The process also helps prevent future problems from occurring.

In order to find the root cause, an IT person usually needs to look at data, information, and trends. As stated earlier, most politicians only look at data. By looking only at data and not information, their solutions only fix symptoms. By not looking at trends, their solutions are short sighted and don't fix things for the long term.

If all I do is tell the salesperson to stop writing down credit card numbers, I'm only fixing a symptom. If I only ensure the credit card number is encrypted when written to the database, I'm only fixing a symptom. A root cause analysis may require a complete audit of the entire security system. It would mean asking questions like:

- How do we ensure nobody ever writes down credit card numbers? Should we banish pens and pencils from the workplace?
- Is our company PCI compliant?
- Are the expiration date and PIN stored on the computer system?
- How do we ensure the security of a credit card number as it moves through the IT infrastructure?

A root cause analysis doesn't just fix a symptom, it performs a thorough analysis of the process and related processes. It analyzes the data and how it's stored, whether it's written on paper or stored on a computer system. The root cause analysis objective is to fix all the core problems and ensure that the symptoms won't happen again.

To create a solution to eliminate a problem, though, you first have to define what the problem is. To eradicate poverty, for example, you have to define what "poverty" means.

Here is an excerpt from the U.S Department of Health and Human Services website:

> Are the poverty guidelines before-tax or after-tax? Are they gross income or net income? What definition of income is used with the poverty guidelines?
>
> There is no simple answer to these questions. When determining program eligibility, some agencies compare before-tax income to the poverty guidelines, while other agencies compare after-tax income.

Some government agencies say poverty is based on gross income, while others say it's based upon net income. If the government programs are based on net income and true poverty is based upon gross income, the government will never supply enough funds to lift people out of poverty. The government hasn't defined poverty. The government isn't performing a root cause analysis to understand the problem, so it can never fix the problem.

Politicians are always fixing the same things over and over again because they fix the symptoms and never fix the root cause. Maybe this is because solving a problem would mean they'd be out of a job.

Problem Solving

Problem solving is the process of defining a problem, determining possible solutions, and implementing the best solution. Now we know that defining a problem requires root cause analysis. Finding a solution that fixes the problem without creating new problems is problem solving.

There are three critical aspects to finding solutions.

The first is the ability to "think outside the box." This means to think of solutions that are unique, different, long term, cost-effective, safe, and something most people agree are viable solutions.

The second aspect is to be respectful. When an idea is presented, no matter how stupid it may sound, be respectful and ask for more details. Remember, the idea is an idea; it's not a solution. Many dumb ideas end up evolving into brilliant solutions. If an idea is immediately dismissed as stupid, it's a personal attack on the person who presented the idea. Personal attacks discourage people from speaking up and presenting new ideas.

The third aspect is to think of everything that can go wrong. Once an idea for a solution is presented, how can it be broken? What could go wrong with the solution? What could be the unintended consequences? This is also known as playing devil's advocate. It is critical that the second aspect of being respectful occurs during this phase. If people are trying to break an idea, the person who came up with the idea may feel like their idea is being attacked and may take it personally.

Multiple solutions were implemented to try to ensure the safety of customers' credit card information. We held a class teaching all salespeople the importance of not writing down credit card numbers, what PCI compliance is, and how the computer systems process credit card information. We implemented daily surprise inspections of salespeople's work areas. We performed a thorough audit and found that all the computers, the network, and the database server encrypted the data. We confirmed that the website used Transport Layer Security (this converts the website address from "http" to "https," ensuring data encryption and security when the customer's computer, via the Internet, talks to the company's computers) and that the customer credit card information was encrypted. We confirmed that we were PCI compliant and that we performed monthly automated system security checks.

These solutions didn't just fix the root cause of the problem; they were proactive in preventing future problems. An added benefit was that salespeople could explain to customers how and why their credit card numbers were safe.

Politicians, government agencies, political pundits, and the like rarely apply the three aspects to finding a solution. They only think of solutions that fit their agendas. They aren't respectful of or professional regarding opposing viewpoints. They never have someone play devil's advocate and think of what could go wrong.

The U.S. has had multiple banking crises over the years. There was the 1930s crisis where over 9000 banks failed. There was the 1980s Savings and Loans crisis, and the most recent one, the 2008 crisis. Canada, on the other hand, has never had a banking crisis. In the 1930s, there were two minor Canadian banks that failed. During the 2008 crisis, Canada didn't have any banks that failed.

The trends indicate that Canada has solved the problem of keeping banks financially sound, whereas the U.S. hasn't and keeps repeating the same mistakes over and over.

Efficiency

Efficiency is being able to do more work in less time or with less cost, or both. Lean manufacturing and lean business process development are examples of philosophies on how to improve efficiency. Computers are not the only way to improve efficiency, but they are a great tool to help improve how much work people, departments, and businesses can get done.

Keying a credit card number into a computer system is much more productive than the salesperson writing the credit card number on a piece of paper and keying it in later. However, it isn't more efficient if the credit card entry and processing are not secure.

In 2012, the Department of Veterans Affairs (VA) reported that the average wait time for a veteran to be processed to receive disability benefits was over 270 days. Ninety-seven percent of the veterans had to fill out paperwork to apply for these benefits. If the VA were computerized, it would be able to drastically reduce veterans' waiting times to receive benefits.

Improved efficiencies don't just allow more work to be done in less time or with less cost. They can improve employee morale, make the department or business more flexible, and most importantly increase customer satisfaction. In the above example, the veterans are the customer and the customers are not happy having to wait nine months because the government is inefficient. The veterans deserve better.

Business Knowledge

Business knowledge is a foundational knowledge. It is a basis of understanding that is required on which solutions can be built. As an IT person, I must understand accounting, marketing, manufacturing, distribution, project management, inventory control, customer service, product development, supply chains, e-commerce, logistics, quality control, sales, payroll, human resources, and government regulations.

IT people interact with all functional departments of a business. Business knowledge gives us the foundation to understand what the department does, what its objectives are, and to design systems to help meet those objectives.

Most people don't realize that the government has the same functional departments. For the VA to process benefits, it needs accounting, distribution of services, project management, customer service, quality control, payroll, human services, and government regulations. The VA hospitals need these functional areas, along with inventory control, product development, and supply chains.

The fact that the VA takes nine months to process veterans' benefits is a data point. The fact that many banks failed during the 1930 recession is a data point. The fact that many banks failed during the 2008 recession is a data point. These data points combine into information and imply that politicians don't have the necessary business knowledge, skills, or understanding to create laws to solve the country's problems.

Business Culture

This is a topic most people don't even think about. Business culture is driven by the executive staff. The executive staff has certain goals and moral or social objectives that they want to drive the business toward. However, these are not what make up the business culture. The business culture comes from how the employees react to the executive staffs' actions. Business culture is the ingrained behaviors and values of the employees. For example, if management wants to create a culture where employees present new ideas but management is always telling employees what to do, management isn't creating the culture they said they intended to. In reaction, the employees stop presenting new ideas and the business culture becomes a culture of keeping ideas to oneself.

Implementing a culture requires a vision and consistent actions in enforcing that vision. An IT department's culture stems from customer service. All the other employees in the company are the IT department's customers. We have to create a culture of computer uptime, data security, troubleshooting, open communication, problem solving, honesty, integrity, and many other facets that all are part of a professional attitude toward customer service. If the IT department has the vision of excellent customer service and acts toward that vision, our customers believe that exceptional customer service is part of our department's culture.

Politicians have created a culture where lobbyists spend billions to influence politics. A culture where it's acceptable for veterans to wait nine months to receive benefits. A culture where it's okay for banks to fail during economic crises. A culture where political power is kept for themselves and their party. A culture that is not focused on the American people.

Change Management

Change Management is a process that gets people to accept new computer systems, new procedures, new ideas, and new solutions. People are resistant to change; they are content and secure in believing things that they've always believed. Getting people to change from their current ideas and adapt to and utilize new ideas is a complicated process. The concept is simple, but achieving the change is very difficult.

Implementing change requires explaining what the change is, why it's beneficial, and to keep pushing for the change. A new way of doing things can't just be stated once and people will accept it. It must be communicated from multiple perspectives and multiple angles. The communication and actions must be persistent and reasonable so the new way becomes familiar and comfortable, just like the old ways were.

Democrats and Republicans have shown that they are extremely resistant to change. Each party has its ideologues and philosophies. Neither party shows a willingness to change. Neither party is willing to look to look at the problems and solutions from multiple perspectives. Neither party is willing to change the rules so other political parties and philosophies can gather strength.

As an IT person, I deal with change on a daily basis, and I have learned to embrace change. As I began to dabble in politics, I realized the political world was changing, but not in a way I liked. As I immersed myself further into politics, I instinctively applied my skills and knowledge. I analyzed the facts and information that were being supplied. I looked at trends. I looked to see if there was logic in people's arguments. I wondered what problem the politicians and political experts were trying to solve. I wondered what their experience, knowledge, and motivations were.

As I listened to the experts, I realized I had to stop. I was frustrated. I realized I had a unique and different perspective. Questions kept popping into my head that nobody was answering. Nobody was digging for the truth. Nobody was giving all the facts.

So, I started looking for the answers to my questions. I started searching for facts and the whole truth. As I gathered more data, I analyzed this new data and turned it into information. I kept applying my IT skills against the new data and information. Then, I started thinking of solutions that I've never heard from politicians, political pundits, on political forums, or from political experts.

Then, I wrote this book.

2 What Is an Independent?

In the 1950s, around 20 percent of the population identified themselves as Independents. By 2010, that number had slowly risen to 30 percent. In 2011, that number jumped to 40 percent (31 percent claimed they were Democrats, and 27 percent claimed they were Republicans). Most Independents are partial to one party or the other because of their base beliefs. Independents who lean toward being Republican are usually more fiscally conservative. Independents who lean toward a Democratic ideal are usually more socially liberal.

According to Wikipedia, the definition of an "independent voter" is controversial and fraught with implications (sounds scary and ominous, doesn't it?). According to Rush Limbaugh, the conservative talk radio show host, Independents don't know what they believe. According to the book *The Myth of the Independent Voter*, there is no such thing as an Independent voter. The book claims everyone is either a Democrat or a Republican. On political shows, when a voter claims they are Independent, they are invariably asked "What does that mean?" or "What do you believe in?" All the so-called experts believe that Independents don't know what they believe and aren't really Independents. Or, as Stefan Zweig points out, "The free, independent spirit who commits himself to no dogma and will not decide in favor of any party has no homestead on earth."

If all the above were true, then why, over the last 40 years, has the number of Independents grown? Why do so-called experts claim that Independents don't know what they believe or are a myth, yet many people claim to be Independents? The data doesn't add up.

As I looked at more data, I noticed that as the rift between both parties has grown, so has the number of people who call themselves Independents. As the intellectual dishonesty that emanates from both parties has grown, so has the number of Independents.

What this means is that an Independent's political leanings are irrelevant. It doesn't matter if the Independent votes for one party 40 percent of the time or 80 percent of the time. It doesn't matter if the person is registered with a political party or even votes in the primaries. It's not the political leanings that makes a person an Independent. An Independent is someone who doesn't walk in lockstep with the beliefs of a political party. An Independent is someone who is open-minded. When a new political idea is presented, Independents don't immediately agree or disagree with the idea, regardless of which party stated the idea. Independents hear an idea and (this is the critical point) then listen to the opposing viewpoint. Independents listen to both sides before deciding whether they agree or disagree with the idea.

The number of Independent voters continues to grow because voters are frustrated. It seems Democrats and Republicans haven't just stopped talking with each other; it seems that both parties now hate each other.

Democrats are too busy yelling, screaming, claiming the climate is changing, throwing temper tantrums, picking flowers, picking their noses, having gay sex, screaming "racism," being horrified by big business (but not big government), listening only to lawyers, stating political facts, ignoring true facts, spending more money than they have, being self-righteous, and failing at talk radio to take the time to listen to a Republican.

Republicans are too busy yelling, screaming, claiming religious freedom, throwing temper tantrums, murdering flowers, not washing their hands after peeing, not having sex, screaming "class warfare," being horrified by big government (but not big business), listening only to the 1 percent, stating political facts, ignoring true facts, taking all the money they can get, being self-righteous, and failing at evolving to take the time to listen to a Democrat.

When Democrats and Republicans talk politics, they seem to be emotionally attached and make it personal. They attack the opposing viewpoint. They treat anybody who disagrees with them as villains. They are emotionally attached to their party and their moral righteousness. They are condescending. Talk radio, TV shows, blogs, political forums on the web, and political books are full of Democrats and Republicans who are like this. It seems impossible to find any political radio, TV show, TV station, book, or website that isn't full of emotionally charged, belligerent, condescending, closed-minded know-it-alls who keep spouting their party's talking points.

This is why there is a struggle in understanding what Independents believe. According to political pundits, as soon as a new idea is proposed, if you don't immediately agree or disagree with it, then they believe you don't know what you believe. That you don't understand what is going on. That you aren't getting involved and getting into the fray. That you are standing on the sidelines as a spectator.

Independents do understand what is going on. All political discussions seem to immediately get to a personal level, and people don't feel comfortable in those situations. What most Independents believe is that they would love to have a civilized, intelligent, unemotional, philosophical, theoretical discussion on political topics.

Independents aren't emotionally attached to a moral righteousness or any particular party's ideologies. Independents think. Independents want facts. A wonderful Christopher Hitchens quote sums up the Independent: "The essence of the independent mind lies not in what it thinks, but in how it thinks."

Independents will listen to what Democrats have to say and try to understand why Democrats believe what they do. Independents will also listen to what Republicans have to say and try to understand why Republicans believe what they do. Independents know that if two parties are diametrically opposed on any given topic, then most likely neither party is 100 percent correct. The ability to listen, understand, learn, and try to find faults with their own or anyone else's beliefs is what makes Independents who they are.

The problem and struggle Independents have, is that they don't have information. When Democrats or Republicans express their talking points, they give out only smidgens and fragments of data. They withhold information and build their arguments based on only the data points that support them.

Independents need information in order to make a decision on whether or not they agree with an idea. The information they need is NOT being supplied by any political party, political experts, talk radio, or political forums. One of the primary objectives of this book is to supply the information that Independents crave.

3 Marketing Brand

A marketing brand is the image that a company wants people to have of their product. It may not be the image people have of the product, but it is what the company wants or hopes people have. It is how the company views its product and how it wants you to view their product, with the same passion. Choose your favorite soda pop and think about how much you like it, how you savor it, how it is high quality because every time you open a can of the pop it delivers the flavor you expect. If you don't like pop, choose your favorite restaurant or beer or geek-gadget manufacturer; it doesn't matter.

Now think of the logo of the pop and how whenever you see that logo, it makes you think of the pop. This is part of the "brand" of the pop. The brand is supposed to give you an emotional attachment to the product.

Political parties are no different from a company. Each party tries to create a marketing brand that instills an emotional attachment to the party. Each party's logo is a visual presentation of their brand. The Democrat logo is a donkey, and the Republican logo is an elephant (who the heck picked these logos?).

The Democrat donkey was first used as a logo by Andrew Jackson in 1828 because his opponents called him a jackass. The Republican elephant was first used in a political cartoon in 1874 and labeled "The Republican Vote." Today, the Democrats claim the Donkey is smart and brave while Republicans claim the Elephant is strong and dignified.

Separate from the logos is the brand itself. A brand is similar to a business culture. A political brand starts out as the ideal envisioned by each political party. However, the brand is actually how voters react to the actions of each political party. The key for each political party is to ensure their actions are close enough to their ideals that their own voters still trust the party and believe in the brand.

Democrats have two primary ideals that make up the core of their brand. The first ideal is how Democrats call themselves progressive. Democrats used to call themselves liberal, but that label became an insult after Republicans constantly blasted people for it. So, the term "liberal" became a bad political brand and now Democrats call themselves progressive instead.

Democrats believe "progressive" means "open-minded," open to new ideas and moving forward. They believe the world is constantly changing and that the government has to adapt and change with it. They think that what may have been justifiable in the past does not necessarily hold true today, and what may have been the way of life at one time doesn't mean it should always continue just because it worked then.

There are many examples of how life in the U.S. has evolved and how we have become more morally responsible as a people. Slavery has been abolished, women can vote and work or stay home with the kids, and companies can't discriminate based on color, creed, gender, age or sexual orientation. It is this march forward to better ways of doing things that Democrats consider to be progressive.

The second primary ideal of Democrats is that they like to think of themselves as intellectuals. Intellectuals are people who use intelligence in their daily lives. Intellectuals consider their reasoning and thinking abilities to be higher than the average person's. Intellectuals believe they "think outside the box" and are capable of using logical thought. Democrats truly believe this, especially when they compare themselves to Republicans.

These two ideals help to explain the brand that Democrats try to create. A brand isn't a single statement; it's usually made up of multiple concepts. Here are some of these concepts, put into words, that are used to create the Democrat brand:

- Regulated marketplace
- Government acts as a counterbalance to capitalism
- Friendly and peaceful foreign policy

- Caring and compassionate
- Protectors of society and the environment

Republicans also have two primary ideals that make up the core of their brand. The first ideal is how Republicans call themselves conservatives. Conservative means looking to the old ways for guidance. Keeping tradition intact and not changing things unless they need fixing. The old saying of "If it ain't broke, don't fix it" applies to conservatives. This is why conservatives like smaller government, like it was in the past. Our country didn't have welfare programs for its first 150 years, and it prospered and grew. Our country was the shining beacon of liberty and freedom to the rest of the world. Republicans believe this is based upon the fact that the government was small and didn't interfere with a person's pursuit of happiness.

Republicans' second ideal is that they are the protectors of freedom. Republicans believe if a person works hard, that person should be allowed to enjoy the rewards of their hard work. The government can't and shouldn't take those rewards away. Freedom isn't free, and Republicans take great pride in fighting for a person's right to keep their just rewards and to keep the government from taking all those rewards. Republicans truly believe this whenever Democrats want to make new laws and increase the size of the government.

These two ideals help to explain the brand that Republicans try to create. Here are some of these concepts put into words:

- Small government
- Free marketplace
- Strong military
- Individual rights
- Religious freedom

Independents look at both parties' brands and think, "What a bunch of horse manure." When Independents see the Democrats' logo of a donkey, they think of an ass. When Independents see the Republicans' logo of an elephant, they see a big, unsympathetic, trampling animal.

Donkeys and elephants should be offended that they are being used as logos by the political parties.

During presidential elections, each political party starts talking about appealing to the independent voter. They start talking about moving more toward the center. This is where their brands fall apart. Independents realize that the brand that each political party espouses doesn't match the reality. Independents see that each political party's actions don't match its ideals or brand. Independents' reactions to each political party are actually a true indication of the true brand of each political party.

Independents view Democrats as lovers of big government, fiscally irresponsible, lovers of government greed and power, and untrustworthy. Independents view Republicans as lovers of big business, fiscally irresponsible, socially backward, lovers of business greed and power, and untrustworthy. These aren't all the views Independents have of each party, but swearing just isn't polite.

So what is the Independents' brand? There isn't one. The reason Independents don't have a brand is that there is no party or management team trying to create a brand. This is part of what causes the confusion among Independent voters; there is no brand for Independent voters to become emotionally attached to. Without an Independent brand, it's difficult for either party to understand what Independents believe.

So, let's try to define the Independents' brand. The brand of Independents is a two-sided scale. One side is common sense, balanced by the other side, which is open-mindedness.

Independents weigh the pros and cons, they factor in historical context; what is going on in the world around them currently; society; individual freedom; the government; capitalism; emotions; information; objectives; desired outcomes and expectations; and they listen to both sides of an argument. Okay, so maybe it's a multi-sided scale, but you get the picture.

These are the ideals that make up Independents. I believe the concepts that most accurately reflect the Independent brand are:

- Individual rights weighed against societal rights
- Workers' rights balanced with capitalism
- Minority rights and religious rights
- Efficient government
- Fair marketplace with consideration to society
- Professional military and a consistent foreign policy
- Self-reliance with the added protection of a safety net

If a person who considers himself an Independent doesn't believe in the above brand, that is okay. Independents are just that, Independent. Each Independent is a free-thinking and open-minded person. The term Independent doesn't refer to a political party; it refers to a way of thinking. Some Democrats and Republicans are Independents, they just don't realize it.

Not all Democrats, Republicans, or Independents will fully support the concepts, beliefs, or ideals expressed above or throughout the book. Nor will they support all the solutions that are provided later in the book. Each person may have more of a sliding scale of support for each party, concept, belief, or ideal. What is important is when the terms Democrat, Republican, or Independent are used, they are not taken as absolutes. Do not take these terms as data; think of them as information, as general concepts. Consider it a way of thinking.

Most people have worked for a boss who claims he has an open-door policy and that you can talk to him about anything. You quickly realize the open-door policy doesn't truly exist, and you learn not to trust the boss on many matters. The same is true with political discussions, except *you* could be the boss. As you read this book, if you don't have an open-door policy within your head, then you are part of the problem.

4 Individuals

In Medieval Europe, the individual's role was based upon gender and family. Men who were of noble birth were expected to be protectors and usually owned land. Men who were peasants were expected to be tradesman, hunters, or work the land. Women of noble birth were expected to be pleasant and respectful. Women who were peasants were expected to marry, raise the family, and provide labor to help the husband.

The role of the individual in American society was initially defined in the Declaration of Independence and has evolved to embrace not just individual white men, but all men and women. A relevant quote from the Declaration of Independence is, "We hold these truths to be self-evident, that all men are created equal, that they are endowed by their Creator with certain unalienable Rights, that among these are Life, Liberty, and the pursuit of Happiness."

Life means the right to protect your life and enjoy it. It means your life is your own and is not dictated by whether you are of noble birth or a peasant. Peasants are no longer dependent upon people of noble birth; they are dependent upon themselves.

Liberty means the right to think and take action upon your own judgment. You have the freedom, right, and responsibility for yourself.

Pursuit of Happiness means being a crewmember of the starship Enterprise and living in the Star Trek universe. Okay, maybe not. It means the individual can live for his own sake, not for what others dictate. The individual can pursue what she wants and what makes her happy.

The above aspects of the Declaration of Independence are explained this way because its focus is on the individual, not society. This focus starts to bring up other questions and problems. How does an individual attain these? What if an individual has difficulty taking care of himself? What steps are needed for the individual to really rise to his fullest potential? What if what makes the individual happy goes against society's values? What if it causes conflict in the society? What distinguishes how Democrats, Republicans, and Independents view the individual in our country?

The easiest way to visualize how each party views the individual is to utilize Maslow's Hierarchy of Needs, which has five distinct levels and is depicted as a pyramid. In order to advance to the next level, people have to feel comfortable and confident that their needs have been met from the previous level.

- The 1st level, which is the base level, consists of physiological needs. These are the most basic needs that are vital to survival, such as air, water, food, and sleep.
- The 2nd level of the pyramid includes safety and security. These include steady employment, health care, safe neighborhoods, and shelter.
- The 3rd level is comprised of social needs. These include love, affection, family, and a feeling of belonging.
- The 4th level is for self-esteem needs. These include the need to be satisfied, have personal worth, social recognition, and the feeling of accomplishment.
- The 5th level involves self-actualization needs. These include self-awareness, personal growth, and interest in fulfilling one's potential.

The concept of Life, Liberty, and the Pursuit of Happiness can best be attained if the person reaches level five of Maslow's Hierarchy of Needs. However, the means by which each individual attains each level and eventually attains level five is what distinguishes each party.

For level one, Democrats look to the government. Democrats expect the government to be actively involved in helping individuals with their level one needs. Democrats push for food stamps to help people attain food. They expect government-supplied water (city water). They create homeless shelters so people can get off the streets and get a good night's sleep. They expect the government to make laws that keep the air clean. They fully support social welfare programs.

For level two, Democrats continue looking to the government. They want government jobs, and they want the government to support unions. They want health care for everyone. They want a strong police presence for safer neighborhoods. They specifically created the HUD program to help people attain housing. These and the aforementioned programs all play a part in helping people attain level two.

For levels three and four, Democrats stop looking to the government and start looking to society. They start forming into small societies based upon color, sexual orientation, culture and many other facets. It's within these small societies where they can talk to like-minded people and start to feel a sense of belonging.

For level five, Democrats believe the middle- and higher-income earners have attained this level. They also believe many people attain this level if the person helps his fellow human beings, is a social worker, works for a non-profit organization, works towards a better society, or is a government worker.

The problem with Democrats is that they don't realize how difficult they make it for people to ever learn to attain level five. The reason for this is that for levels one and two, they rely upon the government to help people. If people have to rely on the government, then they only learn reliance on the government, not self-reliance.

Consider the parable, "If you give a man a fish, you feed him for a day. If you teach a man to fish, you feed him for life." Democrats put a lot of emphasis on the "If you give a man a fish, you feed him for a day" part. By making people reliant on the government, you are only providing them with fish. You aren't teaching them to fish; you aren't teaching them self-reliance. You aren't giving people the tools and skills they need to learn to fish. You aren't giving people the chance to have self-respect, independence, and the pride that comes with being self-reliant. By teaching people to demand that the government help them,

Democrats are causing the self-affliction of dependency and the people they are helping may never learn self-reliance.

For level one, Republicans believe that individualism and charities are the best solutions because people have to learn to be self-sufficient. People must rely upon themselves to get educated, get a job, buy their own homes, buy their basic needs, and learn to become self-sufficient. If people are struggling, Republicans prefer that charities help provide their basic needs, not the government.

Republicans despise the government helping people with level one. They believe it is too easy for these people to live off the government, that the people will have no desire or need to work hard, and that they won't strive for self-reliance and independence. An example is unemployment benefits. Republicans want to limit how long people can collect unemployment. They believe people won't look for a job until the unemployment benefits run out.

For level two, Republicans expect individuals to be responsible for their jobs, their health care, and their shelter. However, for security, Republicans rely on individuals and the government. Republicans want individuals to be able to carry guns. Republicans want the government to provide a strong military, an active Homeland Security, and a strong police presence.

For level three, Republicans look to the family and religion. For many Republicans, family and religious gatherings are their safe haven for social interaction.

For levels four and five, Republicans resort to capitalism. Whether a person owns their own business or works for someone else, Republicans like the idea of being responsible for making things happen and the camaraderie of working with other people. It's fulfilling to grow and improve the sales and profits of a business. By working, people are relying upon themselves to meet their needs, and they attain self-reliance.

The problem with Republicans is how they treat people who are struggling to obtain levels one and two. Republicans always seem to want to cut money for food stamps, Social Security, Medicare, and Medicaid. They want charities to help the people, not the government. But charities say they aren't big enough, nor do they have the logistical capabilities to do the job. Charities want the government to do the heavy lifting, and the charities will supplement and fill in where needed.

The other problem with Republicans is that they always want to keep wages down. They always want to reduce or eliminate the minimum wage. Republicans don't want to pay people enough money in wages so that the people don't need the government's help in attaining levels one and two.

Many corporations pay people the minimum wage, and even after the workers have been at the company for years, they are still paid the minimum wage. Many corporations only hire part-time help so they don't have to provide health care, vacations, and retirement benefits. In essence, Republicans and businesses make it extremely difficult for people to attain levels one and two on their own. Many people are forced to turn to the government for help.

In relation to the fish parable, Republicans completely ignore the "If you give a man a fish, you feed him for a day" part. Republicans don't realize you have to feed the person so the person has the strength to learn to fish. The second part of the parable, to a Republican, might be, "If the adult doesn't know how to fish, too bad." Or even, "If a big fishing company comes along and catches all the fish, too bad."

For Independents, the fishing analogy would be completely rephrased, possibly as such: "You must feed a person fish while you teach them the multiple skills needed to catch their own fish. The rewards of fishing must greatly outweigh the ease of being given fish."

In order to attain levels one, two, and three, people must be fed, nurtured, educated, and taken care of if they are struggling. Government guidance, in combination with charities and individual pride, is the best method to attain this. Most people getting government help don't want it, but they don't have a better alternative.

If people are self-motivated and have the means, they won't need the government or charities; they can attain levels one through three themselves. If they don't have the means or are struggling, then the government and charities working together can teach them to learn to be self-sufficient.

Attaining levels four and five comes from within the individual. The government and businesses need to understand that they both can get in the way of this. The government gets in the way by making so many laws and the rules so complicated, people quit striving to go out on their own and start their own businesses. Businesses get in the way by laying people off and destroying their lives. Businesses don't care about the individuals and what damage they cause by taking away a person's paycheck. Big businesses often drive smaller competitors out of business. I understand that this is part of the capitalist way, but how can a small hardware store survive in a town when Super WalMart carries everything they do at half the price?

So why is all this important? Because it explains how Independents actually care about individuals. Democrats mostly focus their efforts on levels one and two. Republicans mostly focus their efforts on levels four and five. Independents are balanced and realize you have to devote the same focus, attention, and understanding to all of Maslow's levels in order to truly help the individuals, society, and the country to grow and prosper.

As you read the rest of the book, keep Maslow's Hierarchy of Needs in mind. Many of the ideas and solutions presented on how Independents would address issues have their roots in Maslow.

I know, I know, I've already asked you to keep an open-door policy in your mind, and now I'm asking you to keep Maslow's Hierarchy of Needs in mind. I will try not to ask you to keep anything else in mind.

5 Society and Morals

Morals play a big part in government and politics. Morals define how Democrats, Republicans, and Independents view many topics like abortion, gay marriage, racism, and even healthcare. The morality of individuals is defined by their beliefs and their society.

When Democrats and Republicans talk of society, it's difficult to understand what society they are referring to. The word society means different things to different people, so to help clarify, we'll break the term "society" down into four separate groups:

Location - Location societies are based on, well, location. The primary locations are neighborhood, city, urban, rural, county, state, or country.

Belief - Belief societies are based on common belief. These include religion, philosophy, politics, teams, and even businesses.

Culture - Culture societies are based on multiple aspects like the color of people's skin, ethnicity, sex, sexual preference, and income.

Combination - Combination societies are comprised of all three societies described above. These include professional organizations, shared interests, shared experiences, and online societies.

Democrats and Republicans agree on most aspects related to the location society and the combination society. They understand that each of these societies has its own perspectives and rights. For example, both Democrats and Republicans agree that the location society of the USA is the land of freedom and opportunity. Part of that freedom is that combination societies such as DemocraticUnderground.com and FreeRepublic.com are free to operate as they choose.

Where Democrats and Republicans really differ is in the Belief and Culture societies.

Democrats' morals are primarily based upon the culture society. Their beliefs stem from the history of the white society persecuting all the other cultural societies. These manifest in the Civil Rights Movement, immigration laws, gay and lesbian pride parades, and many other types of movements. All these movements exist because the different cultural societies have had to fight persecution and have had to fight for equal treatment while existing in the white, male-dominated location society of the USA.

Democrats support the right of a woman to have an abortion. Democrats believe a woman should have the right to choose. The female society should not be told by the male society and the religious society that they can't have an abortion. The fetus is part of the woman's body, and if she decides not to allow it to grow into a baby, that is her choice.

The Supreme Court in Roe v. Wade in 1973 said because of the 14th Amendment and a right to privacy and due process that abortion is allowed (especially during the first trimester). The location society of the USA said that women can have abortions. Democrats are tired of the white male-dominated society and the religious society who keep trying to tell women they can't have an abortion and what they can and cannot do with their own bodies.

Democrats strongly despise racism. Democrats know that racism has existed for a long time and that it still exists today. Racism primarily comes from the white society and is usually directed at the black society, but it can also be directed at many of the other cultural societies. Democrats find racism in any form to be morally reprehensible. As soon as Democrats believe someone is being racist, they immediately speak up and want it known that racism is wrong.

Democrats support a healthcare system that covers everybody. Democrats believe it's wrong that an industrialized society will not provide healthcare for all its citizens. With the current healthcare system, many people who exist in the cultural societies cannot afford healthcare. Democrats believe healthcare is another area where the white male society and the rich society are purposely discriminating against all the other cultural societies, just as they have done for hundreds of years.

The primary problem with Democrats and their beliefs is that they have a tendency to view the world through a culture society prism. Once Democrats believe an issue or topic is related to the culture society, they immediately view the world through the culture society prism and aren't capable of viewing the issue or topic from any other perspective.

The first example of this is how Democrats rarely look at individuals. When Democrats view a person, they view the person by which culture society he or she is a part of. Democrats, when looking at a black Republican, can't understand how a black person can be a member of the Republican society.

Another example of their shortsightedness becomes evident when Democrats are confronted by someone who has a different philosophy from theirs. Many people have issues with President Barack Obama's policies, and have different opinions. Democrats don't see these differing opinions and philosophies directed toward an individual, but as attacks against the culture society of black Americans. Democrats scream "racism" because they only see the culture society, not the difference in philosophy. Democrats assume that the Republicans challenging President Obama's philosophies are racist.

The same holds true for immigration and many other issues. Democrats believe that people who are against immigration are racist. However, most people are NOT against immigration; they are against illegal immigration. There is a huge difference between legal and illegal. Democrats, because of how they view the world through their culture society prism, can't differentiate between legal and illegal immigration.

This culture society driven perspective causes other problems for Democrats, the biggest of which is that they are always blaming white society. If you always blame another society, then you will never solve the problems that exist within the culture societies. The culture societies will always have an excuse for their problems and will never go about solving them.

The best example of this is in the lower-income neighborhoods within a city, usually referred to as "inner city" neighborhoods. These neighborhoods usually have huge problems with gangs, violence, and poverty. Many of these neighborhoods consist of either black or latino cultures. By the way, I know that "black, "latino," and "white" are supposed to be capitalized for political correctness. I am tired of everything having to be PC, so I am using lower case letters in these descriptives to put everyone on a level playing field. Instead of putting programs in place to help end the blight of these neighborhoods, it's easier for Democrats to blame the white society. For decades, Democrats have run the city governments where these problems exist, and yet the problems still exist. It's not white society's fault that these problems still exist; it's the Democrats' fault.

Republican morals come from the religious belief society. Abortion and gay marriage are sins to Republicans.

Republicans find it abhorrent to even consider taking the life of a baby that is growing within a woman's womb. They consider life a gift from God, and to kill that gift of innocent life disgusts them. Gay marriage is a sin as well. According to Republican religious beliefs, marriage is supposed to be between a man and a woman. Here is a quote from the Bible about being gay:

LEV 20:13 "If there is a man who lies with a male as those who lie with a woman, both of them have committed a detestable act; they shall surely be put to death. Their bloodguiltness is upon them."

Republicans view racism as wrong. They know that, historically, racism was caused by the white society, but they believe the country has changed. When racism does occur, Republicans view it as an act of an individual, not as an act of the white society.

Republicans look at healthcare from their belief society as well; to them it's a philosophical problem. Republicans philosophically do not like the government intruding in people's lives. Republicans consider healthcare an individual's responsibility, not society's. Republicans believe every time the government creates a program, it's taking people's freedoms of choice away.

There are three primary problems with Republicans and their view of society and morals. The first is that Republicans view the world through a belief society prism. Republicans start pushing their belief society morals on the rest of the country and completely ignore their belief of individual freedom. Abortion is a single individual woman's choice. Gay marriage is a choice by two individuals.

By viewing the world through their belief society prism, Republicans stop believing in individual rights and freedoms. To Republicans, their belief society of religious morals is more important than an individual's rights.

The second problem with Republicans is that they push their religious moral beliefs on society but only use the Bible verses that support their agendas. You never hear Republicans stating that women should remain quiet and submissive, as with this quote:

Timothy 2:12 "I do not permit a woman to teach or to exercise authority over a man; rather, she is to remain quiet."

And what about this quote from the Bible?

James 4:11-12
"Do not speak evil against one another, brothers. The one who speaks against a brother or judges his brother, speaks evil against the law and judges the law. But if you judge the law, you are not a doer of the law but a judge. There is only one lawgiver and judge, he who is able to save and to destroy. But who are you to judge your neighbor?"

Another quote from the Bible you don't often hear in a campaign speech:

Joshua 6-20 & 21
"When the trumpets sounded, the army shouted, and at the sound of the trumpet, when the men gave a loud shout, the wall collapsed; so

everyone charged straight in, and they took the city. **21** They devoted the city to the LORD and destroyed with the sword every living thing in it—men and women, young and old, cattle, sheep and donkeys."

Republicans often use the Bible as data to prove their righteousness. It contains countless passages for moral guidance, but it was written in a very different time. Following it literally is tantamount to Islamic extremists using passages of the Koran to justify violent terrorism. When people single out certain passages from religious texts to further their agendas against their fellow human beings, they are missing the point of God altogether.

If the Republican party wants to use the Bible as a moral compass, then they should use the entire Bible, not just the parts they choose. There are approximately ten verses in the Bible related to homosexuality, but around twenty verses related to not judging other people. Republicans shouldn't be judging whether or not homosexuality is a sin because judging people is a sin. According to these bible verses, Republican men should be telling women to remain quiet. During wars, Republicans should be encouraging the butchering of men and women, young and old, cattle, sheep, and donkeys.

The last problem with Republicans is that they completely ignore and make no attempt to understand the culture societies. The Republican party is made up of mostly white people. The few black people in the party are individuals, not groups or segments of the black culture. When Republicans disagree with President Barack Obama, they don't understand their own cultural bias and cultural ignorance. They don't understand that at times their statements, tone, or body language are racist.

The best example of Republicans' culture society ignorance is their support of the Confederate flag. The Confederate flag is a symbol of the white man's persecution of blacks; it's a symbol of slavery and racism. Republicans will never understand how disgusting the Confederate flag is until they start to understand the culture societies.

Just as Democrats and Republicans are disgusted by the morals of the opposing party, Independents are disgusted by some of the morals of both parties. Independents believe neither party is moral because members of both parties seem to consistently violate their own morals.

Independents find it immoral when Democrats call other people racist when there is a difference in philosophy. Democrats diminish the true ugliness and cruelty of racism.

Democrats don't call out racism whenever it occurs. In 2007, it was a Democrat in reference to Barack Obama who stated, "I mean, you got the first mainstream African-American who is articulate and bright and clean and a nice-looking guy." In 2012, the Democrat who actually made this horrific statement was the vice president.

Independents find it immoral that Republicans only see belief societies and not culture societies. Not caring about the history, persecution, and the issues associated with these cultures is wrong. White men have held power for a long time and don't understand what it's like to live under that boot.

When Republicans try to push their religious morals onto individuals, they're going against the very foundations of the country and its morals and beliefs about the rights of the individual.

Independents' morals come from the understanding that there are four groups of societies and there has to be a balance between the rights of society and the rights of the individual. Independents support abortion and gay marriage because they are individual choices and freedoms. They don't hurt or impede upon any other individual's freedoms, and they don't hurt society.

Regarding healthcare, Independents understand it's a complicated and nuanced issue. Healthcare is a service that has a large economic impact on society. The modes of delivery of healthcare are complex and have very serious ramifications if the service provided isn't professional and efficient. From a moral standpoint, Independents believe that a safety net for healthcare for people who cannot afford it makes perfect sense.

Independents believe that as a society we should take care of our veterans and our elderly. Morally, it's not right to deny these services to people just because they cannot afford the service. Without proper healthcare, individuals can die. This is a serious consequence to the individual and society.

Independents understand that when the U.S. was founded, there were few if any laws to protect society. As the country has evolved, its morals have evolved and it has added many laws to protect individuals and society. The Independent voter's society will continue to evolve and change, but one thing will never change. Independents will always see the closed-mindedness that exists within the Democratic and Republican societies.

6 Promote the General Welfare

"We the People of the United States, in Order to form a more perfect Union, establish Justice, insure domestic Tranquility, provide for the common defence, promote the general Welfare, and secure the Blessings of Liberty to ourselves and our Posterity, do ordain and establish this Constitution for the United States of America."

This, of course, is the preamble to the U.S. Constitution (don't you get chills whenever you read it?). It was written in 1789 to state the intentions of the Founding Fathers in what they hoped to achieve within the U.S. Constitution. If you notice, there are key words that are capitalized; this implies the founders wanted to put emphasis on these words.

The U.S. Constitution was signed and went into effect in 1789. The Bill of Rights is made up of the first 10 amendments to the U.S. Constitution. They were written in 1789, but they weren't fully ratified by three-fourths of the states until 1791.

To understand how Democrats, Republicans, and Independents view the interrelationship between the government, society and individuals, it's easiest to focus on the Bill of Rights and two sentences in the preamble. They are: "promote the general Welfare" and "secure the Blessings of Liberty to ourselves and our Posterity."

Democrats view the government as a force for good. They look at history and see how the government ended slavery. The government gave blacks and women the right to vote. The government passed laws that made discrimination illegal based upon color, sex, or national origin. In 1935, the government passed the Social Security Act, which gave people a chance to enjoy some type of retirement. In 1937, the government passed the Fair Labor Standards Act, which established a minimum wage and made it illegal to have children working.

In essence, the government has made laws that protect the non-powerful from the powerful. The government has made laws that establish a minimum level of safety and security for all citizens. This is why Democrats view the government as good; they believe the government has been a social force that has helped society evolve and grow.

Democrats believe the purpose of the Bill of Rights is to protect people's freedoms and protect an individual's rights. Democrats believe that the government must play a role in providing this protection.

Democrats believe that the world can be a hard place to live in and that life can be unfair. Democrats believe it is morally imperative that the government help people from the horrors of being hungry, thirsty, not having shelter, or having an illness. Democrats believe that by the government providing these services, they are promoting the general welfare.

Democrats believe these welfare programs are "rights." Democrats point to other countries and the United Nations as examples of how these social programs are "rights." The Universal Declaration of Human Rights was adopted by the U.N. in 1948. Article 22 states:

"Everyone, as a member of society, has the right to Social Security and is entitled to realization, through national effort and international co-operation and in accordance with the organization and resources of each State, of the economic, social and cultural rights indispensable for his dignity and the free development of his personality."

Democrats believe that "promoting the general welfare" is a key component of "securing the blessings of liberty." If people are hungry, thirsty, have no shelter, or no security, they can't have freedom and liberty. A person's basic survival needs must be met before a person can partake in "the blessings of liberty."

The first problem with Democrats' beliefs is that they think the government is good and that it did all the good things Democrats believe it did. What Democrats don't understand is that the government allowed slavery, the government allowed people to be discriminated against, the government allowed children to work in sweatshops, and the government allowed businesses to pay almost nothing in wages.

It wasn't until there was a social uprising that the general public demanded that the government change. It wasn't the government that was good, it was the people and society who were good and demanded that the government change. Howard Zinn's book *A People's History of the United States* explains the concept that it is people's actions that are important. It is the people within the society who decide whether the country will be good or not. The people forced the government to act upon the their will to change and make new laws that protect them.

In 2013, multiple government scandals were uncovered that should never have existed. The government was illegally viewing emails, accessing phone records, and monitoring news organizations. These activities occurred because the government was too big and evil and wasn't concerned about following the Constitution. Historically, the government has always allowed the abuse of people and society; it's not until society demands that the government stop do these abuses cease.

Another problem with Democrats' beliefs is their understanding of the Bill of Rights. Democrats believe the Bill of Rights is to protect people's freedoms and protect individual's rights. The question Democrats can't answer is, "Who do people's freedoms need to be protected from?" If the government is so good, who is the threat?

When the country was founded, the true purpose of the Bill of Rights was to protect people from the government. There is a huge difference between believing the purpose of the Bill of Rights is to protect your freedoms versus the true purpose, which is to protect your freedoms from being taken away by the government. It is a total and complete paradigm shift. The government is no longer a force for good; it is now a force for evil, power, and greed that people must be protected from.

Think about the first three amendments to the constitution; the freedom of speech, the right to keep and bear arms, and conditions for the quarters of soldiers. These three and all the rest protect people from a powerful, overbearing, and overreaching government.

Democrats like gun control. In many Democratically controlled cities, it used to be illegal to own guns. But the 2nd amendment was purposefully written to protect people from the government and not allow the government to confiscate their guns. The Pennsylvania Constitution, signed in 1776, stated, "That the people have a right to bear arms for the defence of themselves and the state." This document had a huge influence and was a major precursor to the U.S. Constitution.

In modern times, many tyrannical governments were run by dictators that made owning guns illegal. These include Stalin, Mussolini, and Castro. History is full of governments claiming their desire is to help people, but instead they slowly and methodically create more and more laws and eventually take away all the freedoms in the society. Taking guns away from people makes it so the people can't fight back.

In 1942, Hitler stated, "The most foolish mistake we could possibly make would be to permit the conquered Eastern peoples to have arms. History teaches that all conquerors who have allowed their subject races to carry arms have prepared their own downfall by doing so."

Democrats have done a great marketing job in making government programs sound caring, loving, peaceful and compassionate. But there are many problems with these government programs. The first is that Democrats have gone from "promoting the general welfare" to the fact that they are now "providing the general welfare."

Look at Social Security. The government takes money away from people as they earn it, then when the person reaches retirement age the government doles it back out. Many senior citizens are dependent upon Social Security for their retirement. Without this money, they could not acquire their basic needs of food, clothing, water, and shelter. These people are no longer self-sufficient, nor do they have their own money; they are dependent upon the government for money.

This leads to the next problem of how Democrats perceive "securing the blessings of liberty." Democrats are correct that "promoting the general welfare" and "securing the blessings of liberty" are intertwined. However, people who are dependent upon the government are not free, and they have no liberty. If a person has to get money from the government to meet their basic needs, they have not secured the blessings of liberty. A government that provides the general welfare can also take that general welfare away. A truly free person has their own money and doesn't have to rely on the government. Remember, the government is breaking the law by spying on American citizens. Why can't the government also break the law and stop providing Social Security?

The Democrats continue to use the "provide the general welfare" tactic as a way to take away people's right to choose. Did you ever notice how Democratic politicians always say that evil Republicans want to cut spending on welfare programs and cut Social Security? They do this to get people to vote for them. Democrats threaten and scare people to vote for them. This tactic eliminates people's ability to secure the blessings of liberty. This tactic is not caring and compassionate.

The final problem related to Democrats' beliefs is that Social Security and government-provided welfare programs are "rights." Currently, every taxpayer in the country has to contribute to Social Security. People cannot opt out of paying Social Security. Democrats do not understand what rights truly are.

If something is a right, then people have the right to do it. More importantly, if something is a right, people have the right NOT to do it. If something is a right, people have the right to say no. Consider the 2nd amendment, which says:

"A well regulated Militia, being necessary to the security of a free State, the right of the people to keep and bear arms, shall not be infringed."

The 2nd amendment says that people have the right to bear arms. It also states that gun ownership is necessary to "provide for the common defense" and is necessary for "the security of a free State." When the Constitution was written, a 'state' was the term used for what we now call a 'country.' This implies it is socially responsible of every person to own a gun to provide security for the country. However, because owning guns is a *right*, it also means that people have the right to NOT own guns. Can you imagine the outcry if Democrats were forced to buy guns because the 2nd amendment says gun ownership is a 'right,' and therefore everyone has to participate and must buy guns?

Social Security, healthcare, and all the welfare programs are not rights; they are moral decisions that the location society of the USA has made. They are the programs that the USA has put into place to try and help people who struggle to meet basic needs.

Republicans view the government as a necessary evil. The government is a giant black hole where tax dollars go in, but not much of value comes out. They don't trust the government to do what is right. They believe the government takes away people's freedoms and takes away their ability to prosper. Republicans believe that the smaller the government, the better off the country is.

Republicans view the Bill of Rights as a means to protect individuals from the government. Republicans perceive the government to represent the power and greed that drives most governments. The Bill of Rights was the counterweight against big, powerful government and protected the citizens from it.

To Republicans, "promoting the general welfare" means that the government should get out of the way and leave the marketplace and capitalism to operate with little or no intervention. It means allowing individuals to strive on their own to better their own lives, within the capitalistic system. Consider how Republicans are always complaining that when the government raises the minimum wage, it eliminates jobs, implying that it hurts the general welfare. Republicans believe the government hurts the general welfare whenever it enacts new laws that have an impact on the marketplace.

To Republicans, "securing the blessings of liberty to ourselves and our posterity" means "freedom from the government" for us and our forbears. Freedom is being safe and secure from the government. Freedom is having the right to do as one pleases, as long as it doesn't harm others. Republicans believe that by keeping the government small, it helps keep the government from intruding on people's liberties.

From a Republican perspective, Social Security is a program that should be a safety net; it should be something that everyone does not have to participate in. Social Security is a good program for people that require it, but if people don't require it, they shouldn't have to participate. Republicans would like nothing better than to change Social Security into an optional program, and people can opt out of the program if they wish. Liberty is doing what one pleases, and if people are forced by the government to do things they don't want to do, the government is taking away the person's freedoms and liberty.

The first problem with Republicans is that they don't practice their beliefs that the government is a necessary evil. Republican presidents, with usually a Democratic congress, have signed into law some of the largest government programs that exist. These include the EPA (isn't this ironic?), prescription drugs for Medicare, the Occupational Safety and Health Administration (OSHA), the Consumer Product Safety Commission (CPSC), NASA, the Americans with Disabilities Act, and the Reconstruction Finance Corp (corporate welfare).

In the last 40 years, with a Republican as the President the government has averaged a six percent increase in growth. This is the same average growth rate under Democratic Presidents. Ronald Reagan, who is a god amongst Republicans who believe in small government, increased spending just like a Democrat.

Ronald Reagan was president from 1981 to 1989.

In 1981, the government spent $194 billion on defense, $69 billion on welfare, $153 billion on pensions, and $66 billion on healthcare.

In 1989, the government spent $343 billion on defense, $88 billion on welfare, $248 billion on pensions, and $133 billion on healthcare.

This means that military spending grew at an annual rate of seven percent, welfare at three percent, pensions at six percent, and healthcare at an alarming rate of almost nine percent (note: these numbers are not adjusted for inflation). The U.S. debt went from $1 trillion to $2.8 trillion, which is an average annual increase of 24 percent.

From 1981 to 1989, the U.S. debt as a percentage of Gross Domestic Product (GDP) went from 33 percent to 53 percent. The U.S. government grew at a much faster rate than the economy under Reagan.

Another problem with Republicans is that the country has changed in the last 225 years and they haven't really noticed. When the country was founded, governments were the source of power. However, a new source of power and greed and corruption has arisen that never existed before.

This new source of power is large businesses. Businesses that need thousands of workers in order to thrive and grow. These businesses and their place in power started truly manifesting in our country during the Industrial Age. Power was shifting from the government to businesses, and the businesses abused their power just like the government did.

When Republicans talk about the free marketplace, what they are really saying is they want to "Ignore the general welfare" instead of wanting to "Promote the general welfare."

One example of this happened in 1906, when the author Upton Sinclair wrote the book *The Jungle.* The book exposed how truly horrid businesses in the meatpacking industry were treating workers and producing contaminated food, were unsanitary, or didn't care about worker safety. The book caused a national uproar, and sales of prepared meats tumbled.

In 1906, the government enacted the Meat Inspection Act and Pure Food and Drug Act to ensure businesses produced safe and uncontaminated food. After the passage of these laws, sales of prepared meats returned to normal. The government regulations actually helped the businesses sell their products because people were now assured the products were safe.

Another example of how the Republicans "ignore the general welfare" is the Fair Labor Standards Act. Before this law, the average work day was 11-16 hours and work-related injuries and deaths were common. As was mentioned earlier, the law was created in 1937 to establish a minimum wage, create overtime pay, and protect children in the workplace. Without a minimum-wage law in force today, some wages in America could easily drop down to $5 an hour and children could be working instead of attending school. Some of the 2012 Republican presidential candidates even stated that they thought this would be acceptable.

The final example of Republicans preferring to 'ignore the general welfare' happened during the 2012 Presidential race. Many Republicans running for President in 2012 talked about eliminating the EPA (and Big Bird). America now has clean air, water, and land thanks to the EPA. Before the EPA existed, businesses could do as they wanted and industrial runoff ran directly into the rivers people fished, swam, and drank from. Businesses were dumping toxins, destroying the environment, and killing people. The EPA saved the general welfare from the free marketplace and the greed of businesses.

The last problem with Republican beliefs is that many times their opposition to government laws is in direct opposition to their religious beliefs and the Bible. For example, the minimum wage law ensures people have enough income to meet their essential needs and not live in poverty. Republicans are against the minimum wage law; yet, according to the Bible, they should be helping the poor. Consider Deuteronomy 15:11:

"For there will never cease to be poor in the land. Therefore I command you, 'You shall open wide your hand to your brother, to the needy and to the poor, in your land.'"

Then again, the Bible also says, in Deuteronomy 15:4:

"However, there should be no poor among you, for in the land the LORD your God is giving you to possess as your inheritance, he will richly bless you."

Independents believe that government can get out of control if there are no checks and balances. A government can provide good to the society, and it can be evil as well. A too-powerful and too-large government stifles freedoms and society.

Independents believe that capitalism can get out of control if there are no checks and balances. Capitalism can provide good to the society, and it can be evil as well. A too-small and weak government allows the powerful and wealthy capitalists to abuse the people and hurt society.

In a 2012 Rasmussen poll, 68 percent of the population believed that the government and businesses work in collusion against the individual. This is scary. This shows that something is wrong in both the government and with capitalism within the country. The power and wealth is being kept by the government and the wealthy.

Independents realize that Republicans and Democrats are turning the government slowly into a force of evil and are ruining the country for individuals and society. Independents realize that the number of business lobbyists has more than doubled since 2000 and business lobbyists and government officials interact through a revolving door. Many government officials retire and become highly paid business lobbyists. The businesses, business lobbyists, and government officials are all working together to make laws that benefit the businesses, not the people or our society.

Independents realize that the future of the country is at stake, and if society doesn't push the government to change and start working for the people and society, the prospects of liberty and the hope for a positive future will continue to dwindle. The powerful government and the powerful businesses do not work for society; they work for themselves.

Independents have studied American history and know that many mistakes have been made. Independents believe that in order to "promote the general welfare and secure the blessings of liberty to ourselves and our posterity," you have to create balanced solutions that factor in the strengths and weaknesses of the government and the strengths and weaknesses of capitalism.

Independents know that Democrats and Republicans aren't solving the problems. They know that often, Democrats and Republicans are making things worse. Independents don't know what solutions might work; they just know that there has to be a better way. Never fear, the IT Nerd is here! Enter, the solution.

7 Solving the Country's Problems

"Insanity is doing the same thing over and over again and expecting a different result."

This phrase is attributed to Albert Einstein, but there is no definitive proof that he actually said this. The phrase does a good job of describing the current government and political environment, whoever said it.

In a 2013 poll, 66 percent of Americans had strong concerns about the difference between the rich and the poor. Yet Americans are hesitant to have the government do anything about it. This is not a contradiction, but an example of how little Americans trust the government to solve problems.

For decades, Democrats and Republicans have been trying to solve the country's problems. The following trends show just how poor a job both parties have done in implementing solutions that actually fix problems.

A couple of trends related to Democrats:

Democrats believe that putting more money into the schools will result in a better education for our children. In most subjects, 17-year-old student scores in 2010 were no higher than they were 40 years ago. In 1974, the national average for high school graduation rates was 75 percent. In 2000, it was 67 percent, and in 2010 it had risen back to 75 percent. The trend shows that high school graduation rates haven't really changed; yet, in the last 40 years, the cost to educate each child has more than doubled, after adjusting for inflation.

Democrats have waged a war on poverty for the last 40 years. In 1970, the poverty rate was 12 percent. In 2005, the poverty rate was 12.6 percent. During the depression of 2010, the poverty rate rose to 14.3 percent. This is one trend. Another trend is that the population has increased from 200 million to 300 million.

The important trend is that, in 1970, there were 24 million people living in poverty. In 2010, even if the poverty level had remained at 12 percent, that would mean 36 million people were living in poverty. In 2010, at a 14 percent rate, that's 42 million people living in poverty. This is the true problem and why the Democrats' war on poverty is a failure. Democrats keep pushing for more and more government programs to reduce poverty, but the number of people living in poverty keeps increasing.

A couple trends related to Republicans:

In 1982, Republicans started their "Just Say No" anti-drugs campaign. In 1990, around 20.5 million people used marijuana illegally. In 2010, around 25 million people used marijuana (some legally, and some illegally). In 1982, 32 percent of the population had tried marijuana; in 2012, 38 percent had tried it. There are many other charts and figures that show the fluctuations of drug abuse over the last 40 years. The primary piece of information is that the 30-year war on drugs hasn't reduced the number of people using marijuana and other hard drugs.

In 2010, there were 2.2 million people incarcerated (local, state, and federal); over 500,000 were for drug-related crimes. More than half the federal prisoners were in for drug-related crimes. The U.S. has 743 people in jail per 100,000 citizens. In comparison, Europe averages only 100 people in jail per 100,000 citizens. The percentage of the population in jail in the U.S. is the highest in the world! (Woohoo, we're number 1!) Combining the two trends shows where the real problem lies. The primary result of the war on drugs has not lessened drug use but has increased the number of people in jail.

Republicans believe in supply-side economics and claim that a rising tide raises all boats. The wage rates of the middle income and low income classes have barely kept up with inflation over the last 30 years. This is in contrast to high income earners, whose wages have tripled. The Reagan years (the prime years for supply-side economics) started in 1981 with a poverty level of 12.75 percent. When Reagan's term ended in 1989, the poverty level had risen to 13 percent.

Combining the three trends implies supply-side economics didn't benefit anybody except high-income earners.

That's four different, major long-term trends showing that many of the solutions Democrats and Republicans put into place didn't help the majority of people. So, instead of looking at Democrats and Republicans separately, let's look at a program they worked on together.

Democrats and Republicans both supported the Economic Stimulus Act of 2008. In 2008, the American people were told that there were 70,000 bridges that needed to be repaired. That's more than 10 percent of the bridges in the country. The American people were told that part of the Economic Stimulus Act of 2008 would go toward "shovel ready" projects, including bridge repair. In 2013, during his State of the Union address, President Obama stated that Congress needed more money and that there were 70,000 bridges that needed to be repaired. So where did all the Economic Stimulus money from 2008 go? Why are the country's bridges not being fixed?

Democrats and Republicans believe that home ownership is essential for creating stability, personal security, and wealth in the country. From the 1950s to 2007, the overall home value had appreciated at a faster rate than inflation. For the last 20 years, the equity in homes was one of the most important aspects of people's retirement plans. Many people had more equity in their homes than they had in retirement savings. People wanted to utilize their equity and started refinancing or took out home equity loans.

In 2008, the housing market collapsed and the economy sank into a depression the likes of which hadn't been seen since the 1930s.

The Republicans blamed the Democrats for the collapse because of two laws that Democrats passed. The first law was from 1977, when Jimmy Carter passed the Community Reinvestment Act (CRA). Its purpose was to spark financial support in what were considered high-risk areas for loans. It was designed to encourage banks to lend to people in their community even if the people had poor credit. It was part of the solution to ensure that banks were not discriminating against people in minority neighborhoods.

The second law was from November of 1999, when President Clinton signed into law the Gramm Leach Bliley Act. Section VI of the law made changes to the Community Reinvestment Act. The section of the law that Democrats favored required banks to maintain certain quotas of high-risk loans. To meet the quotas, banks had to come up with more and more ways to make loans to people who were high risk. The banks' solutions were no money down and interest only loans.

The Democrats blamed the Republicans for the collapse because of two major changes Republicans pushed for. The first change was in 1999 and was the repeal of the Banking Act of 1933 (Glass/Steagall Act). The Banking Act of 1933 contained banking reforms designed to control speculation by banks. It was enacted during the Great Depression, and its purpose was to stabilize the banking industry, make people secure in knowing that their money was safe in banks, and to help bring the country out of the recession. It separated the financial market functions of commercial and investment banks. Consumer deposits (commercial banks) were to be kept separate from riskier investment markets (investment banks). The theory was that if depositors wanted to be investors, they could invest in riskier markets themselves. By repealing the Banking Act of 1933, Republicans allowed banks to start speculating again.

The second change was also in 1999, and it was to the Gramm Leach Bliley Act. The change allowed banks to compete in riskier markets like securities and loans. Banks could take all the high-risk home loans they were forced to make and start bundling them into securities. Instead of selling one high-risk loan at a time, banks were now selling thousands of loans bundled together as a security. Many banks, not having any government oversight, were able to label these bundled loans as high-yield securities. Because of the profits of these high-yield securities, banks started making more loans to high-risk people, going way above the quotas the government had mandated.

Banks went from reluctantly making risky loans to wanting to make risky loans, and the marketplace went wild. Banks got the smell of greed and profit and ran with it. Government oversight didn't exist, and the free marketplace was wide open to letting banks compete against investment firms for these high-yield securities.

Democrats blame Republicans, and Republicans blame Democrats for the economic collapse of 2008. Independents know it was both parties who #%*#!*% the American people and caused the collapse.

So why do all these bad things seem to happen? Why do all the bad trends of the last 40 years continue to this day? Why aren't solutions being proposed by Democrats and Republicans, solving the country's problems?

What happens is simple. Democratic politicians are motivated to enhance their careers and cater to lobbyists. Democrats' solutions only fix part of the problems. Republican politicians are motivated to enhance their careers and cater to lobbyists. Republican solutions only fix part of the problems. When combined into a law, the "total package" has a marketing name that sounds appealing to voters, political handouts, and piecemeal fixes, but it doesn't fix the problems. The politicians have no understanding of root cause analysis and no motivation to fix the real problem.

Let's look at each party's solutions in relation to the trends.

It seems that the only solution for Democrats is to keep increasing the size of the government and increase government spending.

- To fix education, they want to increase government spending.
- To help with poverty, they want to increase government spending.
- To try to get the country out of the economic recession of 2008, the Democrats' solution was to spend more government money.

Increasing government spending isn't fixing the problems. The Democrats' solutions are only increasing the size of the government.

The bigger the government, the less efficient it is and the bureaucracy becomes so huge and inefficient that it can't fix anything.

Republicans take a different approach to solving the country's problems. If the problem is something they believe the government is responsible for, they willingly increase government spending. Examples include military spending and drug enforcement.

For almost all other problems, the Republicans' solution is to decrease the size of the government, reduce taxes, and reduce the number of regulations the government imposes. All of these are so the marketplace can run free and theoretically solve the problems.

- To help fight crime, they want to increase government spending.
- To help with poverty, they want to reduce government intrusion and let market forces dictate wages.
- To improve the economy, they want to reduce government spending, cut taxes, and let the free marketplace drive the economy.

Increasing government spending doesn't fix the problems. Decreasing the size of the government and reducing the number of government regulations and letting the marketplace sort things out isn't fixing the problems.

In 2012, four years after the recession started, the country was still in a recession. The unemployment rate was still above eight percent. Hundreds of thousands of people were still losing their homes. The value of houses was still sinking. Democrats and Republicans were still bickering, pointing fingers, and blaming each other for the country's problems (is it any wonder the number of Independent voters is growing?).

Democrats and Republicans have always said and continue saying that the problems are complex and that it is very difficult to solve all of them.

This just isn't true. It's not the problems that are complex; it's the solutions Democrats and Republicans propose that are complex. Democrats and Republicans are closed-minded to new ideas. Democrats and Republicans are too set in their ways and ideals. They don't understand the difference between data and information, they aren't logical, they don't understand efficiency, they don't know what root cause analysis is, they don't do trends analysis, and they aren't capable of thinking outside the box.

Independents know parts of the system are broken. It's time to improve the system. It's time to create a system that changes the rules and makes it so the government is actually capable of creating long-term solutions that protect the country and solve problems. It's a seven-step system, and it's not that complicated.

1) Take the Republican idea of conservatism and apply it

Conservative means if the system works, it doesn't need to be changed. The government has done a good job of passing laws that clean up the environment and giving minorities rights. These programs work, so the first step is to understand why programs work and apply what is learned. Understand history, understand the thinking that went into creating solutions that have worked, and understand the current process, systems, and solutions.

2) Identify what *doesn't* work

Democrats always want more government, Republicans always want less government and more of a free marketplace. Neither of these all-encompassing solutions works. They have been miserable failures. There has to be a balance between too much and too little government. This can't be determined until people understand what didn't work and why it didn't work. In normal terminology, it means learning from your mistakes.

3) Take the Democratic idea of liberalism and apply it

Liberal means being open-minded and looking for new solutions. Liberal does not mean always wanting more government or always wanting less government; it means thinking outside the box. It means finding solutions that have clear objectives, rules, and things that haven't been tried.

Try prototyping. Let states try different solutions, and then determine which solutions work best and use them as a template for the rest of the country.

Understand the strengths of the government and the strengths of the marketplace. Try creating a hybrid system that utilizes the strengths of both.

4) Perform root cause analysis

Root cause analysis is fixing the problem at its core. As in the words of the great philosopher Shrek, "Problems are like onions; they have layers." Democrats and Republicans only fix the outer layers of the problem; they never get to the core of the onion, and they never actually fix the problem.

5) Define objectives, and then propose solutions

The objectives define what the solution is supposed to fix. The objectives need to be SMART (Specific, Measurable, Attainable, Relevant, and Time-bound). The objectives need to define "why" the problem is being fixed.

After objectives are defined, brainstorm to propose solutions. The solutions have to address everything mentioned in the previous four steps.

Creating solutions isn't easy. Computers are a tool. A whiteboard is a tool. In IT meetings, when we are trying to solve problems and come up with solutions, I insist on having a whiteboard available. When trying to solve problems, a person has multiple things going on in their brain. They have their understanding of the problem, they have what-ifs going on to analyze the problem, they have concepts or ideas on how to solve the problem going on. All of these things are swirling around in the person's brain. The same thing is also going on with all the other people in the meeting.

A whiteboard allows a person to take the mishmash of swirling thoughts and project it from her brain onto the whiteboard (sadly, we don't have 3D projectors like in *Iron Man*). The whiteboard allows every person in the meeting to now see the same picture. The whiteboard is a tool that encourages the team to collaborate, communicate, think outside the box, propose new ideas, draw up what-if scenarios, present multiple solutions, and play devil's advocate. The whiteboard is a tool to help create solutions that have the best chance of being long-term successes.

6) Play devil's advocate

Playing the devil's advocate means finding flaws in the solution. It doesn't matter if the solution is your own solution or someone else's. See if there are any reasons why the solution can't be turned into a law. Look at the solution from all different angles and see if there are any things in the solution that didn't factor in to the previous five steps. See if there are hidden agendas, figure out if there are any long-term side effects or consequences. Maybe the ideas have to be combined to create a better solution. See if the law favors some businesses or people over other businesses or people. Try to break the law. Then go back and rinse and repeat all six steps until you are sure of the solution.

7) Information and monitoring

Information is power. Many of the problems the country has are due to things that society isn't aware of. Creating an information superhighway that allows society to quickly and easily ascertain what is going on in and around the government, businesses, and other entities would give the people the information about what's going on behind those closed Congressional doors. Information gives power to the people.

Monitoring is a continuing process that assesses the objectives outlined in step five and ensures that all the objectives are being met. If the objectives are not being met, the monitoring entity has the ability to raise red flags and try to put corrections in place. There is a saying, "You can't improve it if you can't measure it." This is the step to measure performance and determine if the solutions are fixing the problems and meeting the objectives.

Democrats and Republicans create laws, but they never monitor the results, they never see if the results are what they were expecting. If you don't monitor the results, you can never improve the plan. Democrats and Republicans keep offering the same solutions over and over again, expecting different results. Democrats and Republicans are insane.

Below is one possible way by which the government can improve its ability to create laws that truly solve problems.

Create a Voter's Jury that reviews all laws before they are signed.
- This jury consists of 12 people who would be affected by the law.
- This jury has recommendation powers only; they can't change the laws.
- The jury has 90 days to review a law.
- No law can be signed prior to jury review unless there is a two-thirds congressional approval of the law (this covers emergency situations).

  The benefits of this solution are:
- The jury consists of the government's customers. It gives the customers a voice and power.
- The government can no longer sneak laws through.
- The government is now held accountable.

8 Socialism

Socialism is a word Republicans love to throw around. Anytime Democrats make a proposal, Republicans love to say they are being Socialists. Democrats try to downplay that they are being Socialists and believe they are just trying to do the right thing.

If you try searching on the Internet for the definition of Socialism, the results don't help clarify what Socialism is. Some sites call it an economic system, other sites call it a type of government.

Which is it? The answer is, it's both. Socialism is an economic system that involves societal ownership of the means of production. To most people, the societal ownership aspect of Socialism usually means government ownership. Hence, the confusion. Most people don't realize there are other types of societal ownership, outside of the government.

There are three types of Socialism:

1) Cooperative Ownership
2) Common Ownership
3) Government Ownership

Cooperative ownerships are created to share the risks or burdens of running a business. Cooperatives can be non-profit, but they are usually not-for-profit. Not-for-profit means they don't rely on donations but instead rely on the income they generate from the goods or services they provide. However, their goal isn't to generate profits; their goal is to meet their members' needs. For example, a farming co-op supplies farming equipment to plant, fertilize, harvest, and store the crops. Instead of each farmer having his own individual equipment and storage facilities, they share both. The farmers are cooperating with each other to share the risks.

Common ownerships don't pursue profits either. Common ownerships pursue ideas or have a common objective outside of pursuing profits. The three most common common ownerships are non-profit organizations, unions, and shared technology companies (companies that are formed by multiple companies to do research and development, the fruits of which are shared amongst the sponsor companies).

Unions are the only controversial type of common ownership. Democrats love unions; Republicans hate unions. Democrats believe unions protect the workers from bad management and are an absolute necessity to help the working class. Democrats know that unions have been around for a long time and have helped improve wages and benefits for workers.

Republicans despise unions because they are a "society" of workers and the workers should barter for their wages individually. Republicans believe unions are an impediment to an individual's growth, self-worth and to the success of a business.

Independents have mixed emotions about unions. Independents know that unions did serve a purpose long ago in that they protected workers from evil and greedy business people. But the union image has changed. Union management now seems more concerned with itself than it does with the union members (its customers). Over the last 40 years, union membership has dropped from 30 percent of the workforce to 12 percent. Government regulations have made it harder for unions to collectively bargain and hold strikes. But another reason for unions' loss of members is that many union members don't believe they are benefitting from the union. Unions don't have to tell members where their dues are spent, so members don't know if their dues go toward union benefits or to political campaigns or into union management's pockets.

In 2011, the Wisconsin state government passed the Act 10 law; one of the many pieces of this law allowed employees to opt out of the union. The AFSCME (American Federation of State, County, and Municipal Employees) saw its membership in Wisconsin drop from 69,000 to 29,000 members by the end of 2012. The employees who opted out of the union no longer believed in the benefits of being in the union.

Democrats, Republicans, and Independents believe in and support all the remaining types of cooperative and common ownerships (they actually all agree on something. Has hell frozen over? Have the Chicago Cubs won the World Series? Did the world stop spinning?).

Government ownership is the most common form of Socialism, and as stated earlier, what most people understand Socialism to be. The Government pursues creating goods or providing services to meet what the government determines to be the social needs. This form of Socialism includes welfare, Social Security, food stamps, school lunch programs, low income housing, Medicaid, and Medicare.

When the country was founded, government Socialism did not exist in the U.S. The U.S. Constitution does address an "infrastructure" type of Socialism. This includes roads and bridges, the post office, police and fire protection, water and sewage systems, and waterways. These goods and services are managed by the government but are considered vital to the country's infrastructure. These types of Socialism are required for any type of government and so should never be part of the discussion related to Socialism.

Schools were also created as part of the infrastructure type of Socialism, but in a slightly different way. All states required that local communities have schools and that the schools be funded at the local level. However, all students were required to pay a tuition.

The term "Socialism," throughout the rest of this chapter, will refer to the government ownership type of Socialism.

Socialism doesn't rely upon the marketplace to determine what goods and services to provide. Socialism relies on a "central planning" economic model. This is based upon the concept that a central government is better at determining the what, when, how, and cost of goods or services that are being provided. Therefore, Socialism has no intrinsic incentives on finding ways to improve the production of a product or service, improve the quality of the product or service, reduce the cost of the product or service, or improve how to supply the product or service. The only checks and balances in a Socialistic system are the voters. If the government isn't doing its job, then the voters can vote them out and put in place a new set of politicians who will make a new set of false promises.

Democrats believe many goods and services should not have a profit motivation. The benefits provided to society are more important than the pursuit of profits. For Democrats, Socialism is a "socially conscientious" way of providing goods and services.

European-style healthcare is an area where Democrats believe Socialism is at its best. It means that people don't have to worry about any financial ramifications if they require healthcare. It means not putting a price on people's lives. It means taking out the luck factor, in that some people are lucky and don't get sick, whereas other people are unlucky and get sick frequently. People who are unlucky in the U.S. usually end up not being able to afford good healthcare and end up living in poverty and debt all their lives. In essence, Socialism gives up the efficiency and sometimes quality of the service for the safety, security, and well-being of all the people in the society.

The first problem with Democrats' beliefs in Socialism is that they don't work to fix the weaknesses of the system. Socialism is extremely inefficient, there are no incentives to improve the quality or quantity of the service or product. There are no punishments if the quality of the service is poor. If the quality gets worse, there are no consequences.

Remember how it was stated that Veterans Affairs took 270 days to process applications for disability benefits? This sad statistic is a direct result of Socialism and the government not putting processes in place to understand Socialism's weaknesses and addressing them.

Another problem with Socialism is the government is the sole provider and there are no alternatives. There are no repercussions if the government fails to be fiscally responsible, provide a high quality of service, be timely in providing the service, or fails its customers.

The government currently carries an astronomically high debt load. What happens to healthcare if the government stops being able to pay its bills? What services will the government have to cut? What if the government decides to ration healthcare to people who don't support the administration? In a marketplace, there are multiple providers of services. With Socialism, there is only a single provider of services; if that single provider fails to provide the service, the people have no other place to go.

The last problem with Socialism goes back to the issue of freedom. People who are dependent upon the government are not free. People dependent upon the government miss out on the joy of accomplishment that comes with being self-reliant.

Republicans believe that Socialism is evil. They believe governments don't care about anything except getting more power. Republicans believe that a large government is synonymous with Socialism. Republicans believe the government isn't providing the goods and services because it's caring and compassionate, but because the government is in pursuit of power and controlling people's lives. Socialism means more taxes to pay for these goods and services, and the government will take money away from the people who earned it.

Republicans believe Socialism allows the powerful and already established government officials to abuse their power and obtain more power. Republicans believe that the more power the government has, the less freedoms people have. The more people are dependent on the government, the more they will want to stay dependent on the government, making the government more powerful. It's a never-ending circle and eventually will lead to the country becoming so Socialist that it will be on the brink of becoming Communist.

Republicans believe that Socialism lowers the services provided to such a level that everybody is miserable. In a marketplace, if a company provides poor services, it suffers financially and another company will come along to provide better services. With Socialism, no other competition exists, so the government will provide the poorest service it can get away with.

Republicans despise European healthcare. They believe that the services provided in Europe are inferior to the American healthcare system. Republicans present data points that support this claim: cancer mortality rates are 10 percent to 70 percent higher in Europe. Emergency room wait times of two hours or more are 20 percent higher in Europe. Over 40 percent of the population has to wait more than four weeks to see a specialist.

The first problem with Republicans' beliefs is that they fail to see that when Socialism is done properly, it can create safety nets that protect people. People want to be self-reliant, but sometimes bad things happen to good people and they just aren't capable of taking care of themselves. This is where socialized medicine, food stamps, and shelter make sense. As long as these social services are done with the idea of being a safety net only, and not a way of life, they are good for a society.

Another problem with Republicans' beliefs is their support of corporate welfare, which is a type of socialism. Corporate welfare is given out through loans, tax breaks, subsidies, or no-bid government contracts. Republicans support corporate welfare because they believe it provides stability to industries and helps provide a base level of support for these industries. The Farm Bill is a great example of this belief. It helps stabilize corporate farmers, which means a consistent, safe, and reliable supply of food. Republicans support corporate welfare, but not welfare that benefits individuals and society.

Another problem is that Republicans believe in a capitalist healthcare system. The problem is that healthcare doesn't work well in a capitalist system. Capitalism requires people to have time to look at prices, shop around, and determine what providers have the best services for the best prices. The American healthcare system doesn't allow shoppers to do this. Prices aren't posted, and the quality of services isn't posted.

More importantly, when a person has an emergency, they don't have time to shop around, looking for the best healthcare provider; they need a local emergency room. The price is irrelevant to the person needing emergency services and possibly saving their lives, yet it is usually cost-prohibitive.

The American healthcare system is the most expensive in the world. If capitalism were the answer, then America's healthcare system should be the least expensive and most efficient system in the world.

One last thing to consider: isn't people's health too important to be left to a healthcare system whose primary motivation is to make as much profit from the sick person as possible? (What would Jesus say?)

The last problem with Republicans is that they like to blur the line between Socialism, government regulations, and the role of government. Republicans like to call legislation that they disagree with Socialist. Any time the government grows in size, Republicans like to cry, "Socialism!" In 2012, the city of New York banned sugared soft drinks in cups larger than 16 ounces. Republicans called this Socialism run amok. This was not Socialism; it was government regulation. To distort what Socialism means makes it so a meaningful and thoughtful discussion on the topic of Socialism cannot occur.

Independents tire of Democrats saying that Socialism is good. Democrats believe the government is good and that unions are good. A union's purpose is to fight the corruption of management and ensure workers are treated fairly. The government would not have unions if the government were good.

Independents tire of Republicans saying that Socialism is evil. Republicans support the Veterans Affairs hospitals, which offer socialized medicine. If Socialism is evil, the Republicans wouldn't support the VA hospitals.

Independents believe Socialism as a safety net is something that is morally responsible. Socialism does not have market forces to improve efficiency, reduce costs, and improve service, but that doesn't mean that Socialism can't be efficient. Socialism doesn't provide exceptional goods and services, but the goods and services it provides can be adequate to meet needs. Many non-profit organizations are extremely efficient; there is no reason that government-run Socialism can't be as efficient.

Independents know that Socialism can be good or evil; it depends upon the management, the circumstances, the individuals, the needs of society, and many other factors. To Independents, making blanket statements about Socialism doesn't allow problems to be solved.

Independents understand both Democrats and Republicans like and support common socialism, like non-profit organizations. Independents don't understand why neither party comes up with solutions for healthcare, welfare programs, and the many other government programs that could work in conjunction with non-profits. John Hopkins Hospital and the Mayo Clinic are two of the most famous hospitals in the country, and they are non-profit. Independents would learn how these hospitals are run and try to create programs that emulate their success.

Information is the key to making all three types of Socialism successful. Summary level information allows people to make informed decisions on whether an organization is efficient with money, products, and services. It allows people to shop around and determine what organization provides the best products and services for their money. It allows people to put social pressure on an organization to improve the way it runs. It allows people to trust in an organization.

Going back to European healthcare, Independents fully support the idea of all people within a country having healthcare. Independents know that most of the European countries have financial problems because of their healthcare programs. Independents also know that there are some European countries that don't have financial problems and provide exceptional healthcare.

The following are a couple of suggested solutions for improving America's healthcare system. These are not all the solutions and won't fix all the problems. They are presented as a starting point to fixing the healthcare problem in the country.

These same types of solutions can and should be applied to all non-profit organizations, all government Socialism departments, and to almost all government departments.

Healthcare Information Superhighway:

This is a concept that will appear as a solution in other sections of the book. It's a website that anybody can visit and find out about all kinds of information. IT people refer to these types of information as Business Intelligence (BI), Key Performance Indicators (KPI), OLAP cubes (OnLine Analytic Processing), DW (Data Warehouse), Corporate Performance Management (CPM), or TMFA (Too Many Freaking Acronyms).

The objective: give people access to information that is simple to find and easy to understand.

The following needs to occur:
- A government agency is set up that is the gatekeeper of the healthcare industry. This agency manages the Healthcare Information Superhighway (HIS? TMFA?).
- Each medical facility, whether for profit, non-profit, or government-run, is required to report the following information to the above agency and post it on their website: income, expenses, core minor and major medical procedures performed, price of each different type of procedure, price of each medicine, average patient hospital time for each procedure, mortality rates, success rates, and a patient satisfaction survey.
- All insurance companies must report the following information to the above agency and post it on their website: income, expenses, top 10 highest paid executives' salaries, procedures covered, procedures not covered, price of each different procedure covered, and the price of each medicine covered.

The benefits of these solutions are:

- Information is available to the patients to determine what their best choices are for medical services and health insurance companies.
- Competition is fostered in the medical profession, and this pushes medical facilities to perform at an optimal level.

- Competition in the health insurance industry is also encouraged, which pushes health insurance companies to perform at an optimal level.
- Patients can see if the government is efficient and competent in comparison to other medical facilities.
- For-profit health providers are discouraged from performing unnecessary tests to increase profits.

All healthcare facilities are encouraged to become non-profit organizations. Health insurance companies are encouraged to become either non-profit organizations or cooperatives. Government incentives and rewards should be provided for the most efficient and effective healthcare facilities and insurance companies.

9 Accounting and Budgets

In simple terms, accounting is the process of keeping track of the finances of an entity. Budgets are the anticipated income and expenditures over a set amount of time. A budget deficit occurs when expenditures exceed the income.

In the early 2000s, there were a couple of now-famous companies that were involved in accounting scandals. The first company was MCI WorldCom (a telecommunications company), which had sales of over $30 billion. MCI WorldCom used fraudulent accounting methods that showed sales and profits were increasing, when in reality they were decreasing. The scandal broke when it was discovered there was $3.8 billion in fraudulent revenue. MCI was using accounting trickery to spread costs out over multiple years instead of taking the charges in the year they were incurred. This accounting sleight-of-hand allowed MCI to artificially inflate their profit margins and cash flow.

Upon further investigation, auditors learned that the $107 billion in assets that MCI reported equaled, in fact, only $96 billion. That's $11 billion short of the stated value, or around 10 percent. Also, the auditors learned the company had understated their debt load and discovered the true debt load was $41 billion. In summary, the debt load vs. assets ratio was almost 50 percent.

The second company that used fraudulent accounting practices was Enron (an energy and services company). It claimed it had $100 billion in revenue. Enron hid unprofitable businesses and labeled them as "offshore" so they didn't have to include them in their financial statements. Enron purposefully made their financial statements as confusing and convoluted as they could. The accounting firm Arthur Anderson had difficulty navigating through the financial statements and was pressured by Enron to accept the financial statements as they were. Arthur Anderson was supposed to be auditing the business and making sure that all the income was legitimate and all the expenses and debts were legitimate and that nothing was hidden.

The scandal broke, and Enron filed for bankruptcy. To try to prevent this type of fraud from occurring again, the government created the Sarbanes-Oxley Act, which applies only to large, publicly traded companies. This Act increased penalties for fraud and corruption and increased the accountability of the auditing firms.

The government creates annual budgets for each department and then combines them to create the overall government budget. Democrats believe the costs of most government programs increase on an annual basis, and therefore the funding for these programs needs to increase as well.

Democrats believe government agencies should have flexible budgets and the ability to spend what is needed when it is needed. They believe government agencies should have money to maintain services, but they should also have access to more money when it's required.

The Federal Emergency Management Agency (FEMA) is a good example. The country has decided that this agency needs to be prepaid for and must exist at the ready. When an emergency arises, this agency's job is to jump in and help in every way possible. Its immediate goals upon arrival are to save lives and provide resources like food, water, medical care, and shelter. The cost is not nearly as important as the services provided.

Republicans, on the other hand, are inconsistent in their actions when it comes to government budgets. Republicans are consistent when it comes to increasing government military spending. But they are inconsistent when it comes to funding the remaining government agencies. Republicans always increase non-military spending when a Republican is the president. They always want to cut non-military spending when a Democrat is president. This was especially prevalent during the presidencies of Clinton and Obama. Republicans stopped funding the government, caused the government to go into shutdown mode, and only allowed critical government agencies to operate, all in an effort to force the Democratic presidents to reduce the budgets for non-military agencies.

Why Republicans act this way is actually quite simple. Republicans want to cut non-military spending when a Democrat is president because Republicans can claim they are the party of fiscal conservatism. Republicans always increase non-military spending when a Republican is president because then they can claim they are compassionate and caring.

The problem with Democrats and Republicans is that neither party understands fiscal responsibility. The country has been in debt for most of its 200-plus years of existence. However, over the last 40 years the amount of debt has increased dramatically.

Each year, the government is supposed to create a budget. Government budgets are extremely complicated. The Enron and MCI financial statements are simple to understand in comparison to government budgets. This is the first of many problems with the country's debt issues.

Another problem with government budgets is that they make no concession for causality. Causality means that if the number of people who need welfare benefits increases, the budget should increase. It also means that if the number of people who need benefits decreases, the budget should decrease.

The years during most of Ronald Reagan's presidency, from 1981 to 1989, were considered economic boom times. By the end of his term, unemployment was less than 5.5 percent. Most of Bill Clinton's presidency, from 1993 to 2001, was considered an economic boom time. Near the end of his term, unemployment was less than 4.3 percent.

Based upon the above figures, the number of people on welfare should have decreased and the amount of money the government spent on welfare should have stayed the same or decreased. In reality, federal welfare spending from 1981 to 1989 increased from $64 billion to $83 billion. That is almost a four percent increase per year. From 1993 to 2001, federal welfare spending increased from $146 billion to $183 billion. That is an annual increase of three percent per year.

In 1993, approximately 16 percent of the population received some type of welfare benefits. In 2001, approximately 13 percent of the population received welfare benefits. So, from 1993 to 2001, far fewer people required welfare.

Using a rounded population of 300 million, this means the following:

> 48 million received benefits in 1993.
> 39 million received benefits in 2001.

That is a decrease of 18 percent. Eighteen percent fewer people needed welfare, but the budget grew by 25 percent. Where is the causality? Why didn't spending decrease? To make matters worse, there is no government accounting of what percentage of the money actually went to welfare recipients. The government doesn't know if 80 percent or 50 percent or 10 percent of the money in the budget actually went to helping welfare recipients. What was the money used for?

Instead of pointing out each problem, let's just list a lot of data points, information, and trends with government budgets, and you determine whether it's a problem or not.

During the George H. W. Bush presidency, from 1989 to 1993, the number of people who received some type of welfare benefits went from 13 percent to 16 percent. Federal welfare spending increased from $83 billion to $146 billion. That's an annual increase of 15 percent, with a total four-year increase of 75 percent.

In 2010, Medicare's budget was $516 billion. The Government Accounting Office (GAO) reported that Medicare paid $48 billion to the wrong people, for the wrong reasons, or for the wrong amounts. That's $48 billion in fraud, or close to 10 percent of its total budget. This was only fraud, not waste. Waste is from inefficiency, or lost money, or overpaid bureaucrats. Nobody knows how much money is lost or wasted in this department.

There are thousands of departments within the U.S. Government. The GAO is one of these departments. The GAO is responsible for auditing the other government agencies. Their job is to ensure that each government department's accounting is accurate, that they are following procedures, and that there is no fraud occurring.

Isn't the only way that the MCI WorldCom and Enron accounting scandals were discovered was by having outside agencies perform the audits? Why does the government not have outside accounting agencies performing audits of government spending?
Can you imagine a private business that had its own internal accounting department to do all the audits of the company? How trusting would you be of the results of these internal audits? Why is the government allowed to do this? Because Democrats and Republicans allow it.

It gets worse.

In 2006, there were five major agencies that "claimed" they had a total of $797 billion in net assets and $790 billion in costs. These five departments combined are larger than the largest business in the world. These five departments represent over $2500 of each person's tax dollars on an annual basis.

In 2006, the government flunked its annual audit. The auditors were incapable of auditing the books of these five major departments, and most other government agencies (this next part is unbelievable, but true). This was the 10th year in a row that the government's "Consolidated Audit Statement" received a judgment of "No comment" from its auditors. For 10 years, the government can't even audit its own books, even when the auditors are within the government!

The auditors claim that they don't even know what the financial numbers are (isn't this funny? What? Why are you crying? Please don't cry!). At least the auditors are being honest.

The government mandates to businesses that they must pass external financial audits on a yearly basis. The government doesn't mandate the same rules for itself. Democrats and Republicans are almost always willing to increase the government budget, without any financial audits or accountability as to where the money is going. This is worse than what was going on at Enron and MCI WorldCom. This is a blatant disregard for truth, honesty, and the American way. The values of American society are being completely ignored by the government. It's easy to understand why people are turning away from Democrats and Republicans and becoming Independents.

It gets worse.

In 2006, the economy was going good and the government wasn't being fiscally responsible. With the depression of 2008, which financially destroyed families and caused rampant devastation to society, you might think the government would become more fiscally responsible. Families across the world had to cut back, become more conscientious, become more consumer-savvy. So what has the government done?

In January of 2013, the GAO stated that it could not complete an audit of the federal government, making it 16 years in a row that the government could not even audit itself (please stop crying).

The GAO report is 270 pages long and boring as all heck. Instead, here is a summary of some of the findings:

The GAO stated that there were serious problems in the Departments of Defense, Homeland Security, and Social Insurance (Medicare, Medicaid, and Social Security).

The Department of Defense's budget was $799 billion. The accounting practices were so atrocious that the GAO found it impossible to audit.

The Department of Homeland Security's budget was $48 billion. The accounting practices were so atrocious that the GAO found it impossible to audit.

The government promised reductions in Medicare in 2010 through 2012, mainly because of the "Healthcare Plan for America"

(Obamacare). The GAO was unable to "express an opinion" on whether this was true or not.

The government has projected that Social Insurance costs are $27 trillion more than expected revenue over the foreseeable future. The GAO was unable to determine if there was any validity to the current and future costs of Social Insurance.

The report then went on to say that the Federal Government has made significant progress in its financial management since it began preparing financial statements 16 years ago.

So, based upon the above data, the government has been trying for 16 years to get its accounting practices under control. After 16 years, the government still has more than 70 percent of the budget that it still cannot account for in an audit. That's 16 years of Democrats and Republicans not knowing what the @#$%# government has done with trillions and trillions of taxpayer money, while the American people lost their houses, lost their jobs, lost hope, and cried themselves to sleep. The Democrats and Republicans did nothing to bring the government's financial house in order.

It gets worse.

The U.S. national debt is all the money the government owes. It creates bonds that are purchased by its own citizens and by other countries. The U.S. debt as of 2012 was over $14 trillion. That is $46,000 for every American. That is $184,000 for a family of four. The American people don't have this kind of money to pay off this debt.

The largest holders of the U.S. national debt are the Social Security trust funds (16 percent), the Federal Reserve (12 percent), China (8 percent), Japan (7 percent), other foreign nations (19 percent), and money-market funds (6 percent). Over twenty state and federal governments hold another thirteen percent of the debt. Some of these are: the office of Personnel Management, Postal Service retirement, Military retirement, and federal insurance trust funds.

The deficit is the amount of money the government adds to the debt on an annual basis. Just to help clarify: the annual deficit is the amount of money the government is short of each year. The national debt is the accumulation of all the deficits and is the total amount the government owes. The financial budget numbers for the U.S. for 2012 were:

U.S. Tax revenue:	$ 2,170,000,000,000
Federal budget:	$ 3,820,000,000,000
2012 Deficit:	$ 1,650,000,000,000

The government's debt-to-income ratio was 76 percent. Or phrased another way, for every $1 the government took in, it spent $1.76. No business could stay in business very long with this type of annual deficit.

Some Democrats and Republicans started saying that we needed to get the deficit under control and reduce spending. In 2011, there were lots of talks and eventually Democrats and Republicans came up with a compromise that reduced the spending by $38,500,000,000. That sounds like a large number. Democrats and Republicans started giving themselves high-fives and slapping each other on the back, congratulating themselves for cutting spending. But how much did that $38.5 billion really matter? Here is the same budget, with eight zeros removed to put it into terms that Americans can relate to.

Total National Debt:	$142,270
2012 U.S. Tax revenue:	$ 21,700
2012 Fed budget:	$ 38,200
2012 Deficit:	$ 16,500
Budget cuts:	$ 385

So, the high-fives and congratulations were for $385 when the spending needed to be cut by $16,500. If the above numbers were for your own personal family and you needed to reduce spending by $16,500, don't you think you could find some way to save more than $385?

Democrats and Republicans like to say that comparing the federal budget to a household budget is too simplistic. The political forums are especially full of Democrats and Republicans making fun of people who compare the two budgets. But the Democrats and Republicans are wrong. A budget, whether it's for a home, non-profit organization, functional department, business, project, or the government, is still a budget. Democrats and Republicans only make claims about how complicated the government budget is so they don't have to fix the problem.

It gets worse. Try to take deep breaths.

The government isn't learning, the government isn't getting better at managing its money, the government is getting worse. Hurricane Sandy in 2012 devastated the East Coast. FEMA came in and did what it could to help. However, people were clamoring that the government wasn't doing enough. So, the Democrats and Republicans created a Hurricane Sandy Relief bill for $60 billion in extra relief aid. And the Democrats and Republicans were happy. And there was much rejoicing. Some of the provisions in the bill included:

- $4 million for the Kennedy Space Center.
- $20 million for a nationwide "Water Resources Priorities Study."
- $41 million for eight military bases, including Guantanamo Bay.
- $100 million for the federal Head Start day care program.
- $188 million for new Amtrak rail lines (not repairs).
- $5 billion to the Army Corps of Engineers (its annual budget for 2012 was $4.6 billion; this, in essence, doubled that).
- $11 billion for future public transportation projects (not disaster relief reconstruction).

When the bill was finished, only $17 billion went for Hurricane Sandy relief. The Democrats and Republicans took the time to create a bill that had more money for pork and non-emergency projects than it had for emergency relief. If the bill was for emergency relief, it should have passed quickly and gone directly to helping the American people who were devastated by Hurricane Sandy. Obviously, Democrats and Republicans don't care about the American people.

Independents know the government is in shambles. It is fiscally irresponsible, and neither Democrats nor Republicans care. The voters who vote in these politicians don't care either. Independents are smart enough not to buy goods or services from businesses that are corrupt. Independents are smart enough not to support a government that is corrupt.

Independents want financial accountability. They want an effective and efficient government. They want a government that isn't more financially corrupt than Enron or MCI WorldCom. They want a government that is fiscally responsible and doesn't keep borrowing money. They want a government that can quickly help out during an emergency. Independents want the financial insanity of Democrat and Republican spending to stop.

Below are some solutions to start to get the government back to being fiscally responsible.

Government Information Superhighway

This is similar to the Healthcare information superhighway; it's a website that pertains to the whole government, and departments within the government. The objective: give people access to information that is simple to find and understand.

As an IT person, the cost overruns of the Healthcare.gov (Obamacare) website are outrageous. The budgeted cost was $93 million, which sounds reasonable. What isn't reasonable is the actual cost. According to Democrats, the actual cost was over $390 million. According to Republicans, the actual cost was over $1 billion. Either way, the government paid outrageous sums of money for a website that didn't work. The building of the government information superhighway needs to be done efficiently, professionally, and with a management team that actually knows what it is doing.

Some features of the government information superhighway:

- All departments are included, with a hierarchy from the top down.
- Information is available by the common-use name and the department's name. Example: food stamps is the common use name; SNAP is the government name.
- Results of government fiscal audits.
- Government budgets and actual spending.
- Administration costs and the administration cost percentages in comparison to the budgets and actual costs.
- Number of people receiving benefits and average benefits received.
- List of SMART objectives and how well the department performed against the objectives.
- List of measurements of success and how well the department performed against the metrics. Example: All veterans benefit requests will be processed within 10 working days.

The government must become fiscally responsible.

- Each governmental department's budget is frozen until the department can pass a GAO audit.
- Create multiple non-profit organizations that perform audits on the government. Each non-profit would specialize in an area of the government. The results of the GAO audits and the non-profit organizations audits must be published side by side so there are checks and balances on both audits.
- The results of each audit are published on the government information superhighway.

The benefits of these solutions are:

- The government becomes fiscally responsible.
- There are more checks/balances to ensure the government is financially sound. The likelihood of financial corruption within the government is reduced.

There must be a justification of each budget. The government must document at a detailed and summary level the justification for any changes in the budget. The justifications must show solid, relevant, and factual information proving the program's effectiveness and worth. The justifications must show the measurements of success and how well the programs performed against the metrics. The justification must show historical trends and projected trends. This information must be made available on the government's information superhighway.

All funds for projects that are outside of the original intent of the law must be highlighted and added as an addendum to the law. The funds cannot be part of the primary bill and hidden within. One of the jobs of the Voters Jury is to ensure that this process is followed.

Congress and the President cannot increase their pay unless the budget is balanced for the year.

Total federal government spending cannot increase above inflation without voter approval or a two-thirds majority vote by Congress. This allows department budgets to increase faster than inflation if required, but not entire federal government spending.

10 Government Laws & Regulations

The first step in creating a law is proposing a bill. The bill can be proposed in either chamber, the Senate or the House of Representatives. The bill is then sent to a committee. If they approve it, the bill goes to the floor for debate. If it's passed, it's sent to the other chamber, where the process repeats itself.

After each chamber has passed their version of the bill, they have to get together to come up with a combined bill. This can be done by each chamber assigning conferees to a conference committee. The conference committee tries to create a combined bill, which is a bill that is approved by a majority of the conferees on the committee (it doesn't matter how many of the Senate or House conferees approve; just a majority needs to be reached). There are other methods to reconcile the differences between the Senate and the House of Representatives, but this is the preferred method. If a combined bill is agreed upon, then it goes to the President to be signed.

Once a law is passed, the House of Representatives standardizes the text and puts it into the United States Code (USC). The government then authorizes which departments are to create the regulations. These regulations define what is legal and what is not.

The federal government consists of the following departments: agriculture, commerce, defense, education, energy, health and human services, homeland security, interior, justice, labor, state, transportation, treasury, and a few others. At a high level, each of these departments has a clearly defined function/role within the government. It is within these defined functions that the government decides which departments will be responsible for making the regulations.

The department that is responsible for creating the regulations may use many methods and techniques to create the regulations. The first step is to gather information. The agency may ask for outside assistance, other government agency assistance, and/or compare ideas to current government regulations. The second step is to take all the information and write a proposed regulation. The third step is to ask for more input from the same people who contributed to the first step. Eventually, the regulations are finally at a point where they are put into the Code of Federal Regulations (CFR).

The Americans with Disabilities Act (ADA) of 1990 is such a law. The law is considered a civil rights law that, in certain circumstances, prohibits discrimination against people with disabilities. Disabilities are defined in the law as people with physical or mental impairment that limits a major life activity. The law was passed by a Democratic-controlled Congress but signed into law by the Republican President George H.W. Bush.

The ADA law started as a good idea and a good law. But now the regulations have become so complicated and cumbersome that the law has become a huge boon for trial lawyers and a major league headache for the people who have to abide by the law. Here is an example of the regulations for toilet stalls. See if you can figure out what the requirements are.

4.17 Toilet Stalls.
4.17.1 Location. Accessible toilet stalls shall be on an accessible route and shall meet the requirements of 4.17.2 through 4.17.6.
EXCEPTION: Toilet stalls used primarily by children ages 12 and younger shall be permitted to comply with 4.17.7.
4.17.2 Water Closets. Water closets in accessible stalls shall comply with 4.16.
4.17.3* Size and Arrangement. The size and arrangement of the standard toilet stall shall comply with Fig. 30(a), Standard Stall. Standard toilet stalls with a minimum depth of 56 in (1420 mm) (see Fig. 30(a)) shall have wall-mounted water closets. If the depth of a standard toilet stall is increased at least 3 in. (75 mm), then a floor-mounted water closet may be used. Arrangements shown for standard toilet stalls may be reversed to allow either a left- or right-hand approach. Additional stalls shall be provided in conformance with 4.22.4. Appendix Note
EXCEPTION: In instances of alteration work where provision of a standard stall (Fig. 30(a)) is technically infeasible or where plumbing code requirements prevent combining existing stalls to provide space,

either alternate stall (Fig. 30(b)) may be provided in lieu of the standard stall.

4.17.4 Toe Clearances. In standard stalls, the front partition and at least one side partition shall provide a toe clearance of at least 9 in. (230 mm) above the floor. If the depth of the stall is greater than 60 in. (1525 mm), then the toe clearance is not required.

4.17.5* Doors. Toilet stall doors, including door hardware, shall comply with 4.13. If toilet stall approach is from the latch side of the stall door, clearance between the door side of the stall and any obstruction may be reduced to a minimum of 42 in. (1065 mm) (Fig. 30). Appendix Note

4.17.6 Grab Bars. Grab bars complying with the length and positioning shown in Fig. 30(a), (b), (c), and (d) shall be provided. Grab bars may be mounted with any desired method as long as they have a gripping surface at the locations shown and do not obstruct the required clear floor area. Grab bars shall comply with 4.26.

4.17.7* Toilet Stalls for Children. Toilet stalls used primarily by children ages 12 and younger shall comply with 4.17.7 as permitted by 4.17.1. Appendix Note

(1) Water Closets. Water closets in accessible stalls shall comply with 4.16.7.

(2) Size and Arrangement. The size and arrangement of the standard toilet stall shall comply with 4.17.3 and Fig. 30(a), Standard Stall, except that the centerline of water closets shall be 12 in. minimum to 18 in. maximum (305 mm to 455 mm) from the side wall or partition and the minimum depth for stalls with wall-mounted water closets shall be 59 in. (1500 mm). Alternate stalls complying with Fig. 30(b) may be provided where permitted by 4.17.3 except that the stall shall have a minimum depth of 69 in. (1745 mm) where wall-mounted water closets are provided.

(3) Toe Clearances. In standard stalls, the front partition and at least one side partition shall provide a toe clearance of at least 12 in. (305 mm) above the finish floor.

(4) Doors. Toilet stall doors shall comply with 4.17.5.

(5) Grab Bars. Grab bars shall comply with 4.17.6 and the length and positioning shown in Fig. 30(a), (b), (c), and (d) except that grab bars shall be mounted 18 in. minimum to 27 in. maximum (455 mm to 685 mm) above the finish floor measured to the grab bar centerline.

Everyone has used toilet stalls and seen the handicapped stalls with the grab bars. The grab bars make sense and are beneficial for handicapped people. However, just read the requirements for grab bars. In section 4.17.6, it mentions that grab bars must comply with section 4.26, which is a section much later in the regulations. When you get to section 4.17.7.5, which also refers to grab bars, this section refers to section 4.17.6. In essence, the regulations on how grab bars are supposed to be installed are spread throughout the regulations and a person has to keep jumping from one section to another to find all the regulations.

Why aren't the grab bar regulations all in a single section so they are easy to find, understand, and easy for the customer to be in compliance with? How much weight is the grab bar supposed to hold? Where are the figures 30(a), (b), (c), and (d)? What is the purpose, and why is the government writing regulations so convoluted that they are nearly impossible to figure out? Many government regulations are written this way, and it's a problem.

The ADA law doesn't protect businesses that are first-time offenders of any aspect of the law. Lawsuits can be filed without giving the business a chance to become compliant. There is no exact count of the number of lawsuits filed against businesses for not being ADA compliant, but it's estimated that there are at least 25,000 a year.

By Democrats and Republicans writing the law the way they did and the government writing the regulations the way it has, the law is more of a "gotcha" law and many ma-and-pa shops have gone out of business because of the lawsuits. If a law ends up causing just as much harm as it does good, that is a problem. The bad parts of laws like the ADA need to be eliminated, and businesses must be given an opportunity to become compliant with the laws. It is impossible for small businesses to understand or know if they are in 100 percent compliance with a law like ADA.

It's not just government regulations that are confusing, but also how the government communicates to the voters and the instructions it provides for filling out government forms.

During the recession of 2008 and beyond, many homeowners lost their homes and were foreclosed upon. Many of these homeowners were sent 1099c forms from the banks. When a home is foreclosed upon and sold, the losses the bank incurs are offset as profits to the homeowner. For example: If a person owed $100,000 on their home and it was foreclosed upon, the bank would put the home up for auction. If the bank sold the home for $40,000, the bank had a loss of $60,000. According to tax laws, this means the homeowner had a profit of $60,000 and would receive a 1099c for it and have to pay taxes on the income/profit of $60,000. Naturally, this caused a panic in many homeowners, as they had no way to pay taxes on the $60,000 in income. On a side note, common sense would question how the $60,000 is income to the homeowner, but that's what Democrats and Republicans decided.

When filling out federal income taxes, Form 982 needs to be filled out for 1099c types of income. Below are some of the instructions on how to fill out the form:

> Be sure to read the definition of qualified principal residence indebtedness in the instructions for line 1e on page 4. Part or all of your debt may not qualify for the exclusion on line 1e but may qualify for one of the other exclusions.
> 2. Check the box on line 1e.
> 3. Include on line 2 the amount of discharged qualified principal residence indebtedness that is excluded from gross income. Any amount in excess of the excluded amount may result in taxable income. See Pub. 4681 for more information. If you disposed of your residence, you may also be required to recognize a gain on its disposition. For details, see Pub. 523, Selling Your Home.
> 4. If you continue to own your residence after the discharge, enter on line 10b the smaller of (a) the amount of qualified principal residence indebtedness included on line 2 or (b) the basis (generally, your cost plus improvements) of your principal residence.

CAUTION

If the discharge occurs in a title 11 case, you cannot check box 1e. You must check box 1a and complete the form as discussed below under a nonbusiness debt. If you are insolvent (and not in a title 11 case), you can elect to follow the insolvency rules by checking box 1b instead of box 1e and completing the form as discussed below under a nonbusiness debt.

If you are a homeowner, the above instructions are not very helpful in understanding how to fill out the form. However, the next section is included in the middle of the instructions with big letters saying "TIP."

Certain individuals may need to complete only a few lines on Form 982. For example, if you are completing this form because of a discharge of indebtedness on a personal loan (such as a car loan or credit card debt) or a loan for the purchase of your principal residence, follow the chart on page 2 to see which lines you need to complete. Also, see Pub. 4681, Canceled Debts, Foreclosures, Repossessions, and Abandonments, for additional information, including many examples and sample forms.

If you keep digging and can get past the government-speak, you will find some information that is very interesting. If the home foreclosed on is the primary residence of the person, the person doesn't have to pay any taxes on the $60,000 income. The person just has to properly fill out Form 982.

As an IT person, I know how important information is. In the second sentence in the above paragraph, I provided the information that many homeowners were struggling to find. Why isn't the government clearly communicating that if the 1099c applies to a primary residence or the person filed for bankruptcy, the person doesn't have to pay any taxes on the 1099c income? Is it because the government doesn't want the average person to understand the law, and so the person just pays the tax? Current government instructions are written for lawyers to understand; they need to be written so the customers/voters can understand them.

Further reading of government regulations has been known to cause blindness and/or mental meltdown. For your own safety, no more government regulations will appear in this book.

The government keeps growing.

The Code of Federal Regulations (CFR) currently consists of 51 volumes; each volume focuses on a specific area of the government. The CFR contains more than 55,000 pages of government regulations.

Writing government regulations is a primary job for many government workers. In order to keep themselves employed, they need to keep writing and rewriting regulations. There are no incentives for government workers to reduce the size of the CFR. It is to the government workers' advantage to write more regulations, to write them in a way that only they understand, and to write them in the most obscure format they can think of. It's called job security.

Independents know that Democrats and Republicans have written many laws that ignore the needs of voters and small businesses. Independents know that over-complicated laws and regulations and too many laws and regulations stifle the people's ability to be good citizens and be in compliance with rules and regulations created by the government. Independents know that the ridiculous number of regulations keeps small businesses from starting, which hurts the economy. Independents know that if careful deliberation isn't done, the laws and regulations can have unintended consequences.

The Affordable Care Act of 2010, also known as Obamacare, is a great example of just how bad the government is at writing good laws and avoiding unintended consequences. Obamacare was more than 900 pages long (note: some people claimed it was more than 2500 pages long, but that was a gimmick. When printed out in Adobe Acrobat (pdf) format, it was a little over 900 pages long). The Democrats signed it into law in three days. This law (which nobody read because nobody could have read 900 pages of a law in three days) had the following unintended consequences:

- Drug companies could no longer give large discounts on drugs to treat rare medical conditions, even if the malady affected children.

- In 2011, there were more than 700 companies and organizations that asked for and received exceptions to not have to follow the Obamacare law. Everybody else has to follow it, but not the over 700 highly influential companies and organizations.

- Obamacare was touted as a program that would keep health insurance costs down. Before 2012, annual health insurance premiums increased by 10 percent (this is still way higher than inflation). With certain aspects of Obamacare starting in 2012, most health insurance premiums jumped by more than 20 percent. This was double the normal annual increase in premiums. Democrats blame these increases on the insurance companies' greed, but shouldn't this have been foreseen and a solution written into the law to prevent it?

- Obamacare reduced the annual increase for Medicare services to doctors and hospitals. This will require all other people and insurance companies to pick up the slack. This is one of many reasons health insurance premiums jumped by more than 20 percent.

- Under the law, businesses don't have to provide health insurance for those who work less than 30 hours a week. Many businesses that had part-time workers working more than 30 hours a week cut their part-time workers' hours to less than 30 hours a week. The Democratic Party claims it is the party that helps the poor, but that doesn't seem truthful when they are the party that wrote the law that encouraged businesses to cut people's work hours.

Independents know that Obamacare had some good ideas, but it also has a lot of politically motivated ideas. Independents also know that Republicans are just as much to blame for Obamacare as Democrats.

Republicans had control of the House of Representatives, the Senate, and the Presidency for quite a few years prior to 2006. In that time, the Republicans did nothing to help solve the healthcare crisis that was growing in the U.S. Inaction on a problem can be just as damaging to society as a law that takes the wrong actions.

The Democrats and Republicans are only creating more laws and more regulations and are bloating the bureaucracy. The current process is making the government less efficient, less capable of meeting citizens' needs, and less capable of governing in general.

Independents realize that when you analyze government spending in combination with government regulations, the government is a financially bloated, inefficient, unregulated, and uncaring government that doesn't care about its citizens. There are no incentives for the government to improve, and there are no punishments if the government doesn't improve.

Below are some solutions to start getting government laws and regulations to be professional, efficient, advantageous, and understandable to the customers/voters.

Create a "Regulations Jury" that reviews all regulations before they can go into effect.

- This jury would be made up of 12 people; four people who would directly benefit from the law, four people who would be directly and negatively affected by the law, and four people who would not be affected by the law.
- It only takes nine members of the jury to approve regulations.
- The jury can stop the regulations from going into effect and can force the regulations to be rewritten.

The benefits of the jury are:

- The customers of the government feel more secure in the knowledge that regulations should be written in a manner that the customers can abide by.
- Regulations cannot be rewritten just to keep government employees busy.

All companies, organizations, and Congress must follow all laws. Exceptions to any law are not allowed. If any exceptions are needed, then the law is flawed and cannot be passed. This validation of the law would be performed by the Voters Jury.

A process needs to be in place that allows people to query the government for clarifications to laws and regulations. If after documented attempts to get clarification, the person is unable to, the following is allowed:

- The person can request a complete review of the regulations by the Regulations Jury.
- The Regulations Jury can nullify the regulations and send them back to the government for writing.
- The Regulations Jury can cancel all fines, lawsuits, and grievances against the person asking for clarification.

The following rules apply to the person who files for clarification. These rules are intended to ensure that the people/citizens have a voice.

- The person cannot be a lawyer, associated with a law firm, or a lobbyist.
- The person must clearly explain how they were negatively affected by the regulations.
- The person cannot have a net worth of more than $1 million.

All laws must have one-, five- and 15-year SMART objectives. The GAO, as part of its annual audits, determines whether or not the laws are meeting their objectives. If the GAO determines that the law isn't meeting more than 50 percent of the objectives, the government is given one year to rewrite and correct the law. The Voters Jury then reviews the corrections. If after one year the law is not corrected, the Voters Jury can cancel the law.

Six Sigma is a recognized, disciplined methodology used to improve products or services. The government should create a Six Sigma agency that is responsible for cleaning up and modernizing government departments and written regulations. The agency would work in conjunction with the GAO to ensure that laws are meeting their SMART objectives. The agency has a voice in eliminating government departments and regulations that are no longer needed.

Government Laws and Regulations Information Superhighway

This superhighway focuses more on providing information to the people on government performance. It contains:

- All laws and regulations with easy search and navigation.
- What laws have passed the SMART objective review.
- What laws are currently under SMART objective review and the laws' status.
- What the Six Sigma agencies findings have been and what they are working on.
- What regulations are under review by the Regulations Jury.

11 Capitalism

Adam Smith is considered the father of capitalism because of his book *The Wealth of Nations*. When the 900-plus-page book first came out, it was considered too complicated and boring for the general public to read. It sold out in six months. The book is broken down into multiple themes. Many of the themes and ideas expressed in the book have stood the test of time and the changes in economics and are still viable today.

One of the themes in the book was that it wasn't just gold, silver, furs, and spices (i.e. luxury goods) that could make a country wealthy. It was the labor of people who added value to everyday goods and services that could also make a country wealthy. Today, these goods and services are known as our Gross National Product (GNP).

"Labour was the first price, the original purchase - money that was paid for all things. It was not by gold or by silver, but by labour, that all wealth of the world was originally purchased."

However, in order for labor to add wealth to a country, the people who performed the labor had to know that they could personally benefit from their own labor and that those benefits wouldn't be stolen or taken away by the state. People who did the labor did it for their own self-interests, not for the common good of society.

"By pursuing his own interest, he frequently promotes that of the society more effectually than when he really intends to promote it. I have never known much good done by those who affected to trade for the public good.

"It is not from the benevolence of the butcher, the brewer, or the baker that we expect our dinner, but from their regard to their own self-interest. We address ourselves not to their humanity but to their self-love, and never talk to them of our own necessities, but of their advantages."

Adam Smith did not coin the term "capitalism." There is disagreement on who did coin the term. Some attribute the phrase to Karl Marx in his book *The Communist Manifesto.* Karl Marx referred to "capital" and "capitalists" in his writings.

"Capital is money, capital is commodities. By virtue of it being value, it has acquired the occult ability to add value to itself."

"Capitalist production, therefore, develops technology, and the combining together of various processes into a social whole."

In modern society, capitalism is an economic system that allows private ownership. Capitalism consists of owners and workers. It allows individuals and businesses to compete against each other for the creating and selling of goods and services. People have the freedom to determine what to produce, what to price products at, and when to produce them. People who have ambition, brains, and a strong work ethic have the chance to increase their own income and improve the quality of their lives. Capitalism allows people to benefit from their own labor and be self-reliant.

Capitalism is an economic system that relies on a marketplace to buy and sell products or services. It usually relies upon supply and demand for price determination and market forces. Theoretically, it is a system where only the stronger, smarter, better businesses thrive and the weaker ones close up shop. The system provides checks and balances because it is a competitive environment. The system is very effective in ensuring that businesses are constantly looking for ways to reduce costs, improve quality, be more efficient, and keep customers happy.

In America's capitalistic system, there are many types of suppliers. The four primary suppliers are: monopoly, oligopoly, regional, and competitive. Monopoly is when there is only one supplier to the market (example: electrical supply). Oligopoly is when there are only a few suppliers to the market (example: political parties and cell phone companies). Regional is where the people only want to go to regional or local suppliers (example: hospitals, doctors, dentists, and schools). Competitive is when many companies compete to supply goods and services to a very open and competitive marketplace (example: clothing, restaurants, electronics, and appliances).

There are many types of businesses that can exist in a capitalistic system. The three primary types are: sole proprietorship, partnership, and corporation. Sole proprietorship is where there is a single owner of the business. Partnerships have more than one owner and are usually set up as a Limited Liability Corporation (LLC). An LLC allows members to have limited personal liability for the debts or actions of the LLC. Corporations can be private or public. Private corporations are usually owned by a few people, and other people cannot buy its stock. Public corporations allow a portion of their stock to be publicly traded via a stock exchange.

Most Americans believe that capitalism is the best economic system available. They believe it has created the largest middle income class in the world and that anybody in the U.S. can move from being poor to being rich. It is called the "American Dream", and people understand that the dream can be real. It's why so many people from around the world want to immigrate to America (even now). America is the beacon of freedom, prosperity, riches, and not having to live in fear of an oppressive and corrupt government. Many legal immigrants (even from Europe) come to the U.S. so they can start their own business.

Democrats don't trust the concept of a free marketplace within capitalism. Democrats prefer a regulated marketplace. Democrats believe the marketplace needs government oversight to act as a counterbalance to the greed, corruption, and "anything goes" attitude of a marketplace. Government oversight includes building codes, the Consumer Protection Agency, the Environmental Protection Agency, health and safety, protection from discrimination and harassment, and many other oversight type services.

Democrats seem to have a love/hate relationship with businesses. They love businesses that are environmentally friendly, socially responsible, privately held, union friendly, pay their workers well, and are not overly big, greedy, and powerful. Some of these criteria are not quantifiable, but are based more on the perceptions of Democrats. For example, there is no specific criteria for what constitutes an environmentally friendly business. However, if the company is perceived as trying to be green, then Democrats are usually accepting of the company as being environmentally friendly.

Democrats believe companies that make or install solar panels, wind turbines, and other green technologies are good. These companies are reducing the country's dependency on carbon-generating energy sources and are being socially responsible.

Democrats seem to hate businesses that don't meet enough of the perceived criteria. Democrats have been known to call many of these types of businesses evil. Some examples of "evil" businesses are big oil, WalMart, and investment firms.

Democrats believe many investment firms are evil because their sole purpose it to make money. Democrats don't believe these firms are socially responsible because many times after first buying another company, the investment firm fires many of the workers. The investment firm is out to make a profit and isn't concerned about the impact to the workers who have lost their jobs.

Examples of good versus evil companies, according to Democrats, are Costco and Walmart. Democrats love Costco because its average pay is over $20 an hour and new employee pay is above $10 an hour. Also, Costco's CEO makes less than $1 million a year. Democrats hate WalMart because its average pay is less than $13 an hour and new employee pay is close to the minimum wage. Walmart's CEO makes more than $20 million a year. Adding to the dislike of Walmart is that most of Walmart's products are imported from China.

To Democrats, the oil corporations are the epitome of all that is bad with capitalism. Democrats believe these companies are destroying the environment when they drill for oil. If the company has an oil spill, it can devastate the environment. The burning of oil in power plants and gasoline in cars is harmful to the environment.

In 2010, the five largest oil companies added to the hatred by having net profits of $30 billion. To many Democrats, this is obscene. Gasoline prices had skyrocketed at a time when the country was in a recession and workers didn't have extra money to spend. Yet, the oil companies still made massive profits.

Democrats believe all businesses need some type of oversight, but the problem with their beliefs is that they don't believe in the same type of oversight for government. Democrats believe the government can protect society from the greed of businesses. They believe that without government oversight, the businesses would be horribly corrupt, greedy, and not socially responsible. This makes sense. However, there isn't any entity that protects society from the greed of politicians or the government.

Consider the business type of a monopoly. Monopolies have no competition, so the government has to oversee the management of the monopolies so that they provide a reasonable product or service for a fair price. But the government itself is a monopoly. The government has no competition, but there doesn't exist any type of oversight to ensure that the government provides a reasonable product or service for a fair cost to the taxpayer.

Another problem with Democrats' beliefs is their view of what is environmentally friendly. As stated earlier, Democrats don't like oil companies because they believe they aren't environmentally friendly. They discourage oil companies from drilling in the U.S. The oil companies follow the U.S. environmental laws (that Democrats helped pass). By hindering companies' ability to drill in the U.S. in an environmentally friendly manner, Democrats force oil companies to drill in other parts of the world where there are no environmentally friendly laws.

The last problem with Democrats' beliefs is their desire for more laws and regulations. Democrats believe the government isn't doing its job if it's not passing new laws. Democrats wanting to protect the environment and society is a good thing. The problem is that the pettiness and swarms of laws and regulations they feel it is necessary to create stifle the marketplace. As stated earlier, the CFR is more than 55,000 pages long. It is nearly impossible for any person or business to know which regulations they are supposed to follow.

Republicans believe that with capitalism, people have the freedom to choose how to earn a living. Republicans believe capitalism is greed, love, energy, hard work, and most important of all, self-reliance. Republicans believe in the free marketplace and that the marketplace creates competition. Republicans don't believe a business can be too big. Republicans believe that businesses should be left alone and the marketplace should pick the winners and losers.

Republicans believe that government has gotten too big and too intrusive and interferes with the marketplace. Here's a small list of regulations and laws that businesses have to follow: zoning laws, licensing and permits, import/export laws, antitrust laws, income tax laws, sales and use tax laws, patent laws, trademark laws, and OSHA.

The first problem with Republicans' beliefs is that they don't really want competition in the marketplace. Republicans fully support the big companies who buy up the small companies, removing competition from the marketplace. Every time a company is purchased by a larger company, competition is removed from the marketplace. Every time there is a merger of two companies, competition is removed from the marketplace. A free marketplace allows a company to buy up all their competition, turning the business into a monopoly.

Consider this analogy by way of explanation. If the biggest MLB, NBA, or NFL teams were able to buy up all the other teams from all the other cities, there would only be a few owners of all the teams. There wouldn't be any competition. Each year, the owners could pick which team from which city they wanted to win the championship so they could try to keep the fans in each city happy (Hey! the Chicago Cubs could then have a chance of winning a World Series!)

Another problem with Republicans' beliefs is that because of capitalism, the country has more rich and wealthy people than any other country. However, the country also has one of the biggest income disparities of any nation. In many communist countries, the wealth and power reside with the people who run the government. In America, the wealth and power reside with the people who run the government and with the people who run the businesses.

In Communist countries, the top one percent hold over 50 percent of the wealth. In America, the top one percent hold over 40 percent of the wealth. There is a huge disparity of wealth and income in Communist countries and in America.

The final problem with Republicans and their beliefs is that in order for capitalism to pick winners and losers, there have to be losers. In privately held companies, if the company does poorly, the owner loses financially. If the company does well, the owner gains financially. The owner has skin in the game.

The executives of publicly traded companies never lose, therefore there aren't any losers. If a company does well, the executives get nice pay raises and huge bonuses. If the company does so poorly that it has to file for bankruptcy, the executives get huge bonuses to stay with the company to bring it out of bankruptcy. Of course, the working class and the middle class lose their jobs, lose hope, and don't get any money. The only losers when public corporations are run poorly are the employees and the share-holders.

Independents understand why government keeps getting bigger (Socialism) and the rich keep getting richer (Capitalism) and the American citizens keep getting screwed (Realism).

Independents know that government regulations are becoming stifling and limiting the ability of small businesses to thrive and grow. Independents know that many types of regulations are so restrictive that only the large corporations can afford to meet the regulations.

Independents know that the government and large corporations are allowing big corporations to take over the economy. The small businesses are being pushed out, the workers are being left to fend for themselves, and the only winners in the marketplace are the government, public corporations, and the corporate executives.

Independents understand that large businesses carry economic power and have almost colonialism-type attitudes toward com-munities. There are no personal ramifications to executives in large businesses when they close a branch or plant, even though the closure devastates a community. There are no ramifications if they destroy the environment, even though it can make the community dangerous for adults, children, and future generations to live in. There are no ramifications if they promise a new facility and all kinds of jobs and encourage people to move near the new facility and then close the facility a year later, destroying the lives of the people who moved.

A business should be part of a community. A business relies on the infrastructure that society has provided. A business feels safe because it relies on the military that the country has provided. The business products are considered safe to society because the government ensures they are safe. The business relies upon the employees to do the work that allows the business to make money. A business is part of a community, and therefore it must act as a member of the community.

Independents know that capitalism requires laws and regulations where all businesses play by the same rules. The government needs to focus on the quality of the laws and regulations, and not on the quantity. The regulations need to be easy to follow and to act as the gatekeepers for society's safety, health, and benefits. Businesses can focus on profits, but they have to do it within a framework of government regulations that protect society and are morally equivalent to the society's beliefs. The framework still allows business to compete and allows the marketplace to pick the winners and losers.

Some solutions to help create an American capitalistic system that allows competition and also protects society are as follows:

Study countries like Canada and Germany who, in 2012, had flourishing economies. Their economies are based on capitalism, but the government provides social guidance and economic corrections. See how these philosophies can be applied in America.

A company cannot purchase another company if the acquisition makes the company one of the five largest companies in the market sector. Limit the number of acquisitions any company can make to two a year. This makes it so businesses cannot just keep buying up the competition; they have to exist within a competitive marketplace. In essence, strengthen the Sherman Act (which doesn't allow monopolies) and the Clayton and Federal Trade Commission Act (which prohibits monopolistic mergers and anti-competitive mergers).

Give the Voters Jury the added responsibility of ensuring that government laws are designed with the objective of a framework that allows businesses the best potential of growing and succeeding within capitalism while protecting society.

Create laws that make business executives of publicly traded companies financially accountable for business failures (just like small business owners are). If a business files for bankruptcy, some laws could include:

- Executives are not allowed any bonuses or pay raises while the company is in bankruptcy.
- All bonuses and stock options paid to the executives from the previous two years must be paid back to the company.
- The executives must continue working for the company until it climbs out of bankruptcy, unless they are fired. If they are fired, they are not allowed any bonuses or any forms of extra compensation (e.g. golden parachutes).

12 Economics

Classical economics includes a multitude of economic theories during the 18th and 19th Centuries. It promoted economic freedom and the theory that free markets could regulate themselves. As the economy expanded and became more complex, other theories came about. Macroeconomics is economic theory that deals with the overall economy. Microeconomics relates to individual markets or a section of the economy.

Keynesian (John Maynard Keynes) economics (demand side economics) is a macroeconomic theory that came about in 1936, which asserts that demand is the primary key for economic prosperity and the supply side is secondary. Keynesian theory states that by increasing aggregate demand (total demand for all goods and services), you increase job growth and wages, which puts more money back into the economy. With increased demand, the suppliers will increase their production and the cycle continues, growing the economy.

Supply side economics is a macroeconomic theory that came about in the 1970s that asserts that production is the primary key for economic prosperity and that demand is secondary. This theory came about because the economy had had many wild fluctuations in the preceding centuries. Supply side theory postulates that businesses will slowly and steadily reinvest money back into the business. This will keep the macroeconomy running and growing on a more even keel, without the wild fluctuations of demand side economics (it's like a tortoise, not a hare).

To implement supply side economics means reducing the rules, regulations, and taxes on the suppliers. This encourages businesses to spend money on capital improvements like new equipment and any large expense item the business needs. An additional benefit is reduced costs of producing goods or services, and thus the prices of the goods or services will be reduced.

The story of Standard Oil provides a good example of Keynesian theory versus supply side theory, even though the story happened before the macroeconomic theories came about. From the demand side, in the 1870s demand for a new type of oil-based lamp fuel called kerosene was growing. The quality of kerosene fluctuated, and consumers weren't sure if they were buying a quality product or not. John D. Rockefeller saw the value of creating a standardized, high-quality kerosene using a consistent and standardized production process across all his plants. Consumers quickly learned that they could trust this kerosene, sales soared, and the company grew to become the Standard Oil Company. Within a short time, Standard Oil became one of the largest companies in the U.S.

From the supply side, Standard Oil had oil delivered on railroad cars. The railroads were having a hard time delivering enough oil to meet the demand and started raising their rates. Standard Oil then decided to bypass the railroads and invested a lot of money into building a pipeline. Delivery of the oil via pipeline was cheaper, and more oil could be delivered. The pipeline helped increase the supply of oil, and Standard Oil grew even larger.

Supply and demand is a microeconomic theory that explains how changes to the supply or demand impact prices. The four basic rules are:

- If demand stays steady and supply increases, prices go down.
- If demand stays steady and supply decreases, prices go up.
- If supply stays steady and demand decreases, prices go down.
- If supply stays steady and demand increases, prices go up.

Supply and demand are never steady. Here's how the above four rules apply if either the supply or demand changes.

- If supply increases at a faster rate than the demand, prices go down.
- If supply increases at a slower rate than the demand, prices go up.
- If demand increases at a faster rate than the supply, prices go up.

- If demand increases at a slower rate than the supply, prices go down.

Democrats believe in Keynesian economics. Democrats believe that the demand for goods and services has to be provided by the working and middle classes, which make up over 90 percent of the population. Simple logic dictates that if 90 percent of the people start having more spending money, they are going to increase the demand for goods and services.

An example of this is if a single person has an extra million dollars to spend, that person may buy a few high-priced and valuable items. Only a few workers are needed to make these few high-priced items. If 1000 people have an extra $1000 to spend, those 1000 people are going to buy many more goods like televisions, refrigerators, stoves, microwaves, computer games— the list goes on. Many, many workers are needed to make these goods, thus creating a cycle of ever-increasing demand, ever-increasing jobs, and ever-increasing wages.

Democrats believe that the government plays a large role in increasing the demand for goods and services. Democrats believe that government welfare programs give more money to the working class. An example of this occurred in 2010 when Democrats pushed for lengthening unemployment coverage to 99 weeks. Nancy Pelosi, who was Speaker of the House, stated that "Unemployment insurance, the economists tell us, returns $2 for every $1 that is put out there for unemployment insurance." She then continued and said, "It injects demand into the economy, it creates jobs to help reduce the deficit."

Democrats also believe that by taxing the rich and giving the money to the poor, they are helping to increase the demand for goods. Democrats believe that the government helps the economy when it redistributes the money from the wealthy (who won't buy many goods) and gives it to the poor (who will buy many necessities and goods).

Democrats dislike supply side economics and will sometimes refer to it as trickle down economics. They believe that supply side economics only benefits the wealthy. Democrats believe that tax breaks to businesses are not used to invest in capital improvements. Instead, the executives use the money to give themselves raises and keep the money for themselves. The trickle down phrase came about because very little, if any, of the extra tax money trickled back into the businesses or to the workers.

The first problem with Democrats' beliefs is how they've implemented Keynesian economics. Democrats like to use government money to inject more money into the economy. The problem is that government money is money that is already taxed or borrowed and thus has been removed from the economy.

When the government collects $1 in taxes, it has taken the money out of the economy and that money can't be used to purchase goods or services. Demand has decreased. The government can't just transfer that $1 to someone else. The government needs money to run, so the money the government transfers to someone else may only be $.50. The government can't give back the full $1 it already took out of the economy.

Another problem with Democrats' beliefs is that the government is always running a debt, so it has to borrow money from the existing economy to put back into the economy. The government has to pay interest on that borrowed money and has to borrow more than $1 to put $1 into the economy. This is like borrowing money from your child's piggy bank and promising the child you will pay him back. If you don't pay the child back, you didn't borrow the money; you stole it. The government has been stealing from children's piggy banks for a long time.

The final problem with Democrats' beliefs and their understanding of supply and demand is that they don't always practice what they preach. Democrats believe that increasing demand for goods eventually leads to an increase in employment and higher wages. This is true. The problem is that Democrats support illegal immigrants, which increases the supply of labor and lowers labor rates.

Here's how it works. Consider the scenario of three businesses. Each has one job opening, but there are only two unemployed workers. The three businesses have to compete against each other for those two workers, so the workers can demand better wages.

There are 12 million illegal immigrants in the country. In the above scenario, there are now 10 workers applying for those same three job openings. The companies don't have to compete for workers and don't have to pay the workers nearly as much because the workers are desperate and are willing to make less money just to have a job. The illegal immigrants are increasing the supply of workers without any change to the demand for workers, which makes wages go down. It's simple supply and demand, and Democrats are hurting the wage rates of Americans.

Republicans believe in supply side economics, and they believe that supply side economics helps keep inflation in check, helps keep the economy running on a more even keel, keeps businesses profitable and productive, and is the best way to grow the economy out of a recession.

Ronald Reagan used supply side economics to pull the country out of recession. When he first took office, inflation was above 13 percent, unemployment was above nine percent, and the economy was in the midst of another recession. Reagan implemented supply side economics, and by 1985 the inflation rate dropped to three percent and unemployment had dropped to seven percent.

Republicans dislike Keynesian economics because of how it turns into big government trying to create demand. Republicans believe anytime the government is involved, it causes more problems than it solves. By utilizing the government to pump more money into the economy and giving money to the working class, the government is just making the working class more dependent upon the government.

The 1929 recession lasted until World War II. During the 1930s, the government kept trying Keynesian economics. It kept trying to pump more and more money into the economy, but this failed to bring the country out of the recession. When Republicans think back to how quickly supply side economics brought the country out of recession, it just makes them dislike Keynesian economics even more.

The first problem with Republicans' beliefs is their blind support of supply side economics. This was stated in an earlier chapter, but it bears repeating. Reagan made the claim to support supply side economics by saying that, "A rising tide lifts all boats." Considering that supply side economics brought inflation under control and got more people working, it did lift some boats. However, workers' annual incomes rose by only three percent, which barely kept up with inflation. The executives' annual incomes rose by six percent, double that of inflation. The rising tide did not lift all boats equally.

Another problem with Republicans' beliefs is that for the first 200 years, the country relied on classical economics. For a party that claims to be conservative and doesn't like change, they quickly embraced supply side economics. Why would they quickly embrace a new theory when historically they staunchly defended the old ways? The reason for this is that supply side economics benefited businesses and the wealthy.

The final problem with Republicans is that yes, they dislike Keynesian economics, except for when they like it. The military has many programs that are not needed or wanted by the military, but the Republicans keep funding these programs. Republicans love to keep funding unwanted military programs and putting government money back into the economy to benefit their constituents.

Independents understand the different economic systems and the benefits and failures of each system. Independents believe that sometimes supply side economics makes sense and sometimes Keynesian economics makes sense. All forms of tax incentives and tax breaks to businesses are supply side economics. All handouts or extra payments to workers are Keynesian economics.

Independents believe in using supply side economics when trying to change some of the infrastructure of the country. One example is green energy.

The cost to produce green energy is much higher than the cost to produce energy from other sources like oil, gas, and coal, so there wasn't much demand for green energy. The government created tax incentives for companies to produce green energy, which would lower the costs of providing it. Once the costs of providing green energy lowered, the demand for the green energy rose. It took government intervention and regulations to help society become less polluted. Because of these new regulations and government support of supply side economics, many new green energy sources are emerging. Wind turbine farms are sprouting up all over the country. People are insulating their homes and making them more energy efficient. Solar power use is on the rise. Most of these green energy initiatives are the result of supply side economics.

Independents believe that Keynesian economics is where the most benefits are, as long as it focuses on the demand side and not government-provided benefits. Independents support demand economics because they understand supply and demand. If more workers have more money, demand for goods will increase and the prices go up. When prices go up, businesses want to make more money, so they start to increase the supply.

The concept that businesses will increase their supply of goods or services to meet the increase in demand is critical in understanding why demand side economics is so much better than supply side economics. Because of the increase in demand, the supply of the goods or services increases. This means businesses now have to spend more money to buy more equipment, add more office space, and hire more workers so they can increase what they are supplying to the market. Businesses don't need supply side economics to increase capacity and hire workers; they need sufficient demand.

Henry Ford understood the importance of demand side economics, which is why, in 1914, he doubled his workers' pay to $5 an hour. He realized that by paying his workers better, they could afford to buy the products that they were manufacturing and that he in turn would sell more cars and make more money.

Here are some solutions to help create a more stable and socially friendly economy:

On a fundamental level, utilize supply side economics if trying to drive the economy toward a more society friendly goal, like green energy, new technologies, and conservation. Utilize supply side economics to manage inflation and help keep the economy on an even keel. Utilize demand side economics as the foundation to the economy. Use it to increase wages and benefit the people.

Maintain a five percent reserve of the budget that must function within a balanced budget. If the economy is in trouble, the government can tap into the five percent reserve and inject money into the economy. By having a five percent reserve, the government doesn't have to borrow money when the economy needs help. Once the economy has recovered, the government goes back to building up the five percent reserve.

Create tax incentives to encourage businesses to employ full-time American workers. Create tax penalties for jobs that are moved overseas.

13 Wealth & Retirement

Wealth is how much capital or cash reserves a person has. A person's income is their cash flow, while their wealth is their reserves. Wealth is important because once a person stops working, they lose their income and their income is now pulled from their wealth.

Retirement is when a person no longer has to work or can no longer work. The person then has to try to live off the wealth they've accumulated. Before the 1930s, very few Americans had the resources to retire. Most Americans worked as long as they could. The average life expectancy in 1930 was 60 years old. The average life expectancy in 2010 was 79 years old. Because people are living longer, many Americans look forward to being able to retire at 65 years old.

Wealth can exist in many forms. It can be stock holdings, homes, annuities, or even large, valuable collectibles. For most Americans, wealth resides in their home, stocks, bonds, or certificates of deposit (CDs).

In 2010, the top one percent of Americans with wealth owned over 40 percent of the total wealth. The bottom 60 percent, who have little or no wealth, owned less than 2.5 percent of the wealth. There are single Americans who own more wealth than 25 percent of the least wealthy people in the country.

Democrats view excessive wealth as unfair. Democrats believe that most people with excessive wealth have it because they paid their workers poorly and kept all the money. They believe that if a person inherited the wealth, then a previous generation exploited the workers. They believe that most excessively wealthy people are greedy, powerful, and uncaring about society.

Republicans view all wealth as something that is earned. If a person inherits wealth, it was wealth earned by a previous generation. Republicans don't believe there is such a thing as excessive wealth, especially because there is no definition of excessive. Some people may consider $10 million excessively wealthy, whereas other people may believe no amount is excessive. It's a matter of perspective.

Democrats and Republicans believe that every one person should have the chance to retire and enjoy his retirement years. Democrats and Republicans disagree on how people should acquire that wealth. This chapter will temporarily break away from focusing on the beliefs of Democrats and Republicans (and the problems with their beliefs) and just cover wealth and retirement in general.

The government has created multiple programs that are supposed to help Americans have enough wealth to meet their essential needs during retirement. The first program is the Individual Retirement Account (IRA) program. There are pre-tax IRAs, which money can be put into before paying income tax on it. When the individual reaches retirement age, they can pull the money out of the IRA, but they have to pay income tax on the money. The Roth IRA is an IRA into which an individual can put money after paying income tax on it. When the individual reaches retirement age, they can pull the money out of the Roth IRA, but they don't have to pay any income tax on the money.

The next three programs all have one essential ingredient: they all have contributions by the employer and the employee.

The first program is government-run Social Security. Social Security pays money out to the beneficiaries, and any extra tax money collected is put into a trust fund. Social Security came into law in the 1930s and provided benefits once a person reached the age of 65. At the time, the average life expectancy was 60 years old, and over 50 percent of senior citizens lived in poverty. The program's detractors decried it as socialism.

Social Security was the government's solution to the problem of how to take care of people who could no longer work and who didn't have enough money to take care of themselves. It provided a safety net and guaranteed income to meet their basic needs for as long as the person lived.

Social Security is not just a retirement program; it is also a disabilities program. If a person becomes disabled, they can receive Social Security benefits just as if he were retired.

All Social Security money collected that is not paid out to beneficiaries is used to purchase "Special Issue" securities that earn interest. The interest formula was devised in 1960. In 2012, the securities had an interest rate of 1.5 percent.

The second program is a pension plan. There are different types of pension plans, but the primary premise is that the employer and usually the employee contribute to the plan. The plan has a guaranteed return, and the employee is guaranteed so much money when she retires.

Pension plans are managed by a firm that the company pays. Pension plans were designed to encourage employees to stay with a company. The longer an employee worked for a company, the bigger pension they would receive upon retirement.

The last program is the 401k program, which became available in the 1980s and was supposed to act as a supplement to pension plans. The 401k programs were designed to help all employees, not just the executives. The rules stipulate that the highest-paid employees can only contribute based upon the contributions of the average employee. This is why most companies match three to five percent of the contributions of an employee.
Without these matching contributions, most employees would not put money into their 401k plans. Without employees putting money into 401k plans, the executives would not be able to put money into their 401k plans.

401k plans in many businesses have replaced pension plans because they are easier and less costly to manage. With pension plans, if an employee leaves the company, the company still has to manage and pay out the pension. With a 401k plan, the employee usually pulls the money out and moves it to an IRA or their new employer's 401k plan. The original company no longer has the overhead of managing the ex-employee's 401k plan.

As with most government solutions, there are features that work well, but there are also some major problems.

The first problem with Social Security is that it's not funded for the long term. When Social Security started, there were seven workers paying into Social Security for every person who collected benefits from it. In 2010, there were 3.2 workers paying into Social Security for every beneficiary. By 2040, it's estimated that there will be 2.1 workers paying into Social Security for every beneficiary.

The second problem with Social Security is that extra money is supposed to go into a trust fund, and it doesn't. What actually occurs is that the extra funds in Social Security are used to buy special issue government treasury bonds. These bonds can only be purchased by the Social Security Administration. The government takes the extra revenue generated when it sells these special issue bonds to Social Security, and spends it. The government is spending the money that is supposed to be locked away. The government is writing an IOU to Social Security, promising to pay it back.

Another way of understanding it is that the government takes money out of the Social Security piggy bank and spends the money. The government then writes an IOU and puts it into the Social Security piggy bank. Any person who owns piggy banks knows that the money is gone and that an IOU doesn't count as money in a trust fund.

The third problem with Social Security is that it's not the employees' money. If an employee pays the 6.2 percent Social Security tax on their income and then dies right before their retirement, they and their family may never see any of that money.

For example, if a middle income person averaged $40,000 a year in wages over 30 years and had put 6.2 percent into a retirement account that earned a two percent interest rate, they would have over $100,000 of their own money. If the money earned six percent interest, it would amount to over $200,000. When a family has wealth, that money can stay in the family and be handed down to the next generation. This helps a family keep and build wealth through generations. With Social Security, the money isn't passed to the next generation; the money is gone. Social Security doesn't allow a family to build wealth across generations.

The final problem with Social Security is that the taxes are only paid on wages. Social Security taxes are not paid on certain types of bonuses or capital gains. Many companies give out huge bonuses to some managers just to avoid having to pay Social Security taxes. Any wealthy person who doesn't work a regular job and lives off his capital gains never has to pay Social Security taxes. So what happens if the wealthy person becomes sick, loses all their wealth, and becomes disabled?

The primary problem with pension plans is not the plans themselves, but the funding of the plans. Most businesses no longer have pension plans, but all government agencies still do. The government is legally obligated to properly fund pension plans. However, there is no oversight ensuring that the government properly funds the plans. The government oversight that would force businesses to properly fund the plans doesn't exist because the government oversees itself.

The state of Illinois is the perfect example of the government overseeing itself and how this causes problems. In 2012, the Illinois pension plans were underfunded by more than $60 billion. The under-funding was getting to a crisis point because it was going to be difficult to pay the current year's payouts. So, the Illinois legislature did what it had been doing for years: it ignored the problem. There is no government agency issuing fines for under-funding the plan. No elected officials are fired for not funding the plan. There are no consequences for the government not to fund the plan (it's a government monopoly gone wild).

The other problem with government pension plans is that some people receive a full pension after working for just 20 years. Many public officials have been known to work 20 years in one area of the government, then switch careers and work another 20 years in another part of the government. These people can then retire with two pension plans. These people are making more money in retirement than they ever made working. This is not a sustainable process and is one of the reasons many governments have budget problems.

The first problem with 401k plans is that they have become the primary retirement plan for most people. 401k plans are notoriously underfunded by employees. Even if it's in the best interest of the employee to put five percent into the plan and have the company match that, most employees don't. Most employees can't afford the five percent reduction in their take-home pay. Once most Americans reach retirement age, they don't have enough wealth to retire with and become dependent on Social Security.

The other problem with 401k plans is that the money invested is usually in stocks. Most employees don't understand the importance of diversifying. Investing more of your money in stocks at a young age is acceptable, but as a person gets older he should invest more money in bonds and other guaranteed types of investments. In 2008, when the stock market crashed, millions of people lost their retirement money because they had invested it all in stocks. If the money had been in pension plans, the employees would not have lost their retirement money.

Independents believe that building wealth for all Americans is of key, long-term importance to the country. Wealth provides stability and hope. People can draw upon that money when unforeseen costs arise, or to help their kids with college, or to pay for a wedding, or as a down payment on a house, or for any other types of occasions that require extra money.

As important as wealth-building is, the education system does not teach the fundamentals of money management. They don't teach the rule of 72. They don't teach budgeting. They don't teach the value of compound interest.

The rule of 72 is important in understanding wealth building. To know when money will double in value, you divide the interest rate into 72. Earning six percent interest a year divided into 72 means that after 12 years, the money will double. Compared to nine percent interest a year divided into 72 means that after eight years, the money will double. The effects of this rule on a person's wealth can be enormous. This example shows the value of compound interest and the value of a higher interest rate of return. The example starts at $10,000, without adding any more money.

Years	2% Return	6% Return	9% Return
10	$12,190	$17,900	$23,700
20	$14,860	$32,000	$56,000
30	$18,110	$57,400	$132,700
40	$22,080	$102,900	$314,000

Independents know the value of a good education, the value of investing, and the value of money. Independents believe that Social Security should be a safety net, not the primary source of retirement money for many Americans. Pension plans and 401k programs are wealth-building programs, but they need to be enhanced and strengthened so that they become the primary source of wealth and retirement funds for most people.

Some solutions to consider that could help build wealth for all Americans follow:

All businesses that have 20 or more employees and the government must provide 401k plans. They must contribute a minimum of five percent of the employees' pay. Employees making less than $100,000 are required to contribute three percent of their pay. This needs to be done in conjunction with changes to the Social Security tax. The increase in retirement money the employee is forced to put aside is offset by a decrease in the Social Security tax, making it so most employees' net incomes don't change.

Social Security tax must be changed to three percent on all incomes (wages, bonuses, and capital gains) without a cap. If a person earns $1 million in bonuses or capital gains, they have to pay the three percent into Social Security on that money. The Social Security payouts to the beneficiaries remain the same. This means that extremely high income earners are supplementing Social Security to help it stay a long-term and viable program.

The Social Security trust fund must be untouchable by any other government agency. The government cannot spend the money it gets from Social Security when Social Security buys the special issue securities that it is required to purchase. The government must make sure it sets aside enough money to cover the special issue securities and the interest they accumulate.

401k programs must have the option of a guaranteed minimum return of three percent or the rate of inflation, whichever is higher. This makes the program stable and reliable and gives employees a guaranteed amount of money when they retire. Having a minimum isn't hard to implement; many insurance companies already have a guaranteed minimum rate of return of three percent on life insurance policies. This is done because they can earn higher than a three percent rate of return on their investments but only have to pay out a guaranteed three percent.

Tax incentives must be created for investment management firms to help smaller investors who have as little as $10,000 in savings. Investment management firms usually only help people with a portfolio of $250,000 or more. These are not investment advisor firms; many advisors make money based on the amount invested and where it's invested. Investment management firms make money based on how much money the customer makes; it's a different set of values and ethics. Investment management firms manage the investment portfolio of the person so the person doesn't have to. They are professional investors and are usually much better at investing money than people without investing experience.

Schools must teach the rule of 72 and income and wealth building to all high school students.

On an annual basis, businesses and the government must provide a two-hour session on retirement planning for all employees.

14 Income

Disposable income is the amount of income a person has after paying taxes and covering all essential needs like food, clothing, health, and shelter. What constitutes an essential need and the amount of money required to meet an essential need can vary by person. Some people would insist that eating out daily is an essential need. Others may insist that having a 3000-square-foot house with stainless steel appliances, marble countertops and leather furniture is an essential need. Perspectives change wildly depending on what one is used to living with.

The following requirements are basic enough to define as the essential needs of the average American:

- Three healthy meals a day.
- A minimum of 400 square feet of shelter per person with heating, cooling, water, electricity and basic comfort needs met.
- Appliances to cook with, furniture, and some entertainment devices like televisions, computers, etc.
- A telephone or cellular phone for communication and emergencies.
- Fourteen days' worth of clothing, per season.

In 2012, 80 percent of the world's population lived in poverty, making less than $10 a day. With the world's population at 7 billion people, that's 5.6 billion people living in poverty. What Americans consider essential needs, most of the people in the rest of the world consider luxuries.

In the U.S., the poverty line is an amount of income the government believes a person needs in order to meet their essential needs. In 2012, the poverty line for a single person was approximately $11,000; for a married couple, it was $15,000; and for a family of four, it was $23,000. The formula the government uses to calculate the poverty line is how much it costs to feed a person multiplied by three.

This means that a single person spends about $3700 a year on food, and the remaining $7300 covers the rest of their essential needs. A family of four requires $14,800 for food, and the remaining $8200 covers the rest of their essential needs. The government determines what programs and benefits to provide based upon the poverty line.

One major problem with the poverty line formula is that it discourages people from getting married. For example, two people live together and each person makes $15,000 a year. Their combined income is $30,000 a year. If the people are single but living together, their poverty line is a combined $22,000. The government believes these two people are only living $8000 above the poverty line. A married couple's poverty line is $15,000. The government believes the married couple is living $15,000 above the poverty line. The government aid provided to the two people living together is a lot more than the aid provided to the married couple.

There are three different income classes in the U.S. These classes are usually broadly defined, and there is no definitive measurement on what constitutes a person who is poor, middle class, or upper class. To make the issues related to incomes more understandable, let's break the three classes into subgroups and income levels.

The poor make up 31 percent of the population and are broken into two subgroups. The first subgroup is the poor who live near or below the poverty line, which makes up 15 percent of the population. These people struggle daily to have enough money to meet their essential needs. They have no money to help take care of their medical needs, deal with unexpected costs, or take vacations.

The other subgroup is the working poor, which consists of approximately 16 percent of the population. These are people who barely live above the poverty line and have no disposable income. They don't always have enough money to cover their essential needs. Every day is a struggle for them. They don't have any money to cover unexpected costs and never take vacations. They don't buy Nikes and Uggs. They buy generic mac and cheese. These are people who may work one or more part-time jobs or work a full-time job that only pays minimum wage. They rarely have medical insurance.

The middle class makes up 64 percent of the population and is broken into three subgroups. The first subgroup is the working class, which consists of approximately 16 percent of the population. These are people who have very little disposable income. They have enough money to cover their essential needs but struggle to cover unexpected costs, and they rarely take vacations. If they are fortunate, the business they work for helps pay for their medical insurance.

The second subgroup is the mid-middle class, which consists of approximately 35 percent of the population (this is the group most people think of when they think of the middle class). These are people who have some disposable income but live paycheck to paycheck. They have enough money to cover their essential needs, unexpected costs, and can take a vacation every year or so. They don't have much in savings or retirement. If these people lose their jobs, within six months they would become members of the poor. The business they work for helps pay for their medical insurance.

The third subgroup is the upper middle class, which consists of approximately 13 percent of the population. These are people who have lots of disposable income and have healthy savings and retirement accounts. They could live off their savings for more than two years before they would drop to becoming mid-middle class or working class. These people have everything the mid-middle class people do, just more of it and of nicer quality. The business they work for helps pay for their medical insurance.

The executive class (this is a more appropriate name than upper class) makes up the remaining five percent of the population. These people have more money than most Americans can even imagine. These people have annual incomes starting at $175,000 annually, on up to hundreds of millions. Most of these people are better off than the upper middle class, but some are super rich.

Another way to illustrate the classes is to break down the incomes of American households into smaller groupings. In 2009, the income breakout was the following:

- 31 percent of population makes less than $30,000 annually
- Next 28 percent makes between $30,000 - $75,000 annually
- Next 22 percent makes between $75,000 - $100,000 annually
- Next 14 percent makes between $100,000 - $175,000 annually
- Next 4 percent makes greater than $175,000 annually
- Next 0.9 percent makes greater than $380,000 annually
- Top 0.1 percent makes greater than $750,000 annually

The social safety nets are one way society has attempted to help 80 percent of the population meet their essential needs. The poor, the working poor, the working class, and the mid-middle class are the majority of the population who rely on these safety nets, which include food stamps, Medicare, Social Security, Medicaid, welfare, and other programs.

The social safety nets provide a comfort and feeling of security and help people in attaining Maslow's Hierarchy of Needs for levels one and two. However, there is a hidden fear that is always in the back of these people's minds. That fear is the unexpected cost. The unexpected costs can be from medical expenses, appliances breaking down, car repairs, fire, theft, and many other unexpected occurrences that aren't considered essential needs. If an unexpected cost occurs, many of these people don't know how they are going to buy groceries, pay for heating or cooling, or any other essential need.

Democrats believe that the government programs that provide the social safety nets are necessary. These programs allow people to meet their essential needs when they don't have the financial resources to meet them on their own.

Democrats know that many businesses try to pay workers the least amount of money possible. Democrats support the minimum wage law as a way to force businesses to pay a wage that at least covers essential needs. Democrats support unions as a method to help workers get wages that are above minimum wage. Democrats talk about "living" wages, but they never define what that is, nor how they would go about putting laws into place that would force businesses to pay a "living" wage.

Democrats support the members of the executive class who own small- and medium-sized businesses because these people are the entrepreneurs, the risk takers, the builders, and have put their own money into trying to build a business. Democrats despise most of the executive class because they believe that most of the executive class run public corporations and are mostly made up of Republicans.

The first problem with Democrats' beliefs is that they despise the executive class, unless the executive is a Democrat. In 2008, John Edwards was a presidential candidate worth between $20 million and $70 million. Many Hollywood elitists are Democrats worth tens to hundreds of millions of dollars. In 2012, seven of the top 10 wealthiest Congresspeople were Democrats.

A bigger problem with Democrats' beliefs and the programs they support is evident when looking over the last 40 years and the trends. The poverty rates over the last 40 years have fluctuated between 13 and 17 percent, having never fallen below 13 percent.

In 1970, the U.S. population was around 200 million people and 15 percent of the population lived in poverty. That means 30 million people lived in poverty. In 2010, the U.S. population was over 300 million people and 15 percent of the population lived in poverty. That means 45 million people living in poverty.

The government-run social safety nets haven't changed the percentages of people living in poverty. Actually, if you look at the numbers, there are now 15 million more people living in poverty than there were in 1970. The government-run social safety nets may be helping people meet essential needs, but they aren't doing anything to help people get out of poverty and move up to a higher income class.

The last problem with Democrats' beliefs is that they aren't doing anything to increase wage rates to allow people to move up to the middle income class. Democrats keep proposing new government welfare programs or increasing the payouts to existing government welfare programs. The problem is that the poor, the working poor, and the working class don't want to be beholden to the government; they want real wage increases, they want a living wage. They want to share the benefits of all their hard work and increases in worker productivity. It's almost as if Democratic politicians are afraid that if people aren't dependent on the government, they won't vote Democratic.

Republicans believe that businesses should pay workers whatever the market allows. Republicans believe supply and demand should dictate wages, not the government. They believe people are paid based upon the value they bring to the business.

Republicans believe the government spends too much money supporting the social safety nets. Republicans believe that people are learning to turn to the government to help meet their essential needs instead of working harder and trying to make themselves more valuable to the business.

Republicans don't support the minimum wage law because it sets an artificial value on what the worker is bringing to the business. Republicans don't support unions because unions create an artificial value on what the workers bring to the business.

Republicans look down upon unskilled laborers and other types of workers. Republicans believe that if a person is working class, they are not taking ownership of themselves. Republicans believe that everyone should strive to own their own business and set their own destiny. Republicans believe if you aren't striving to better yourself and take ownership of your own financial situation and be your own boss, then you haven't accomplished everything you can. You haven't strived to be all that you can be.

The first problem with Republicans and their beliefs is that every society and business needs workers. Not everyone can be the boss. Just because a worker doesn't want to own their own business or progress up the corporate ladder doesn't mean they are not valuable to the business. In the military, the soldiers are the unskilled laborers and the workers. The generals will gladly tell you that the soldiers are the most important part of the military. The workers are the soldiers of the business world. Republicans should be supporting the workers/soldiers of the business world, just like they claim they support the soldiers of the military.

The second problem with Republicans and their beliefs is that they claim they are pro-family. However, if a single wage earner cannot make enough money to support a family with children, then Republicans are not pro-family. Republicans are forcing moms to have to work, which forces the kids to be raised by daycare centers.

In 2004, George Bush was talking to a divorced mom. He stated "You work three jobs? Uniquely American, isn't it? I mean, that is fantastic that you are doing that." This statement is strongly supported by many Republicans. It's not fantastic that someone has to work three jobs to support a family. A pro-family political party would ensure that a person only has to work one full-time job to support a family. George Bush's statement illustrates just how out of touch Republicans are with the workers and how anti-family they are.

The third problem with Republicans was mentioned in a previous chapter, but it also applies to this chapter. The problem is that Republicans claim to believe people should be personally responsible. People are paid what they are worth and are therefore responsible for how much they make. However, whenever a business fails, the executives don't take personal responsibility. When a company goes into bankruptcy, many workers usually lose their jobs. The executives, on the other hand, are given bonuses to bring the company out of bankruptcy. It seems the only people who have to take personal responsibility are the workers, not the executives.

The final problem with Republicans is that they completely ignore what people need as income to meet their essential needs. Republicans believe that people should be paid based upon their value to the business, not based upon what their essential needs are. Many

Americans today rely on government-run social safety nets because their incomes aren't high enough to meet their essential needs. Republicans are forcing workers to turn to the government to help meet their essential needs. In a way, Republicans are encouraging over 50% of the population to vote for Democrats.

Most people believe that wage rates are based upon supply and demand. What most people don't realize is that there should be an asterisk next to this statement. The asterisk represents the advantage businesses have in the demand side of the equation and how it helps keep wages down. The supply of most types of workers is always greater than the demand for most types of workers. When the unemployment rate was four percent, economists and politicians said it was great. But the four percent means there was a four percent advantage to the demand side, which keeps wages down. The unemployment rate has never been to the advantage of the workers and supply side because the unemployment rate has never been a negative percent.

Another part of the asterisk is that businesses can always go overseas to hire more labor. In the IT industry in the 1990s and 2000s, many companies went to India to hire programmers. The IT unemployment rate skyrocketed because businesses were sending all their programming needs to India.

In Las Vegas, the term "the house advantage" refers to how the odds are always slightly stacked in the casino's favor so that they make more money than they pay out to their gambling customers. The same rule applies to businesses; they have "the business advantage" when it comes to wage rates that are based upon supply and demand.

Independents are disheartened that for the last 40 years, the percentages of the population in each of the six income classes hasn't changed. Neither the Democrats nor the Republicans are doing anything to help Americans improve their financial statuses.

Americans believe that hard work should be rewarded. Worker productivity is a metric that helps define how much value a worker brings to a business. This can be calculated by business, by hour, by state, by country, and by other types of measurements. There are multiple factors that can go into the formula, including part-time workers, full-time workers, and other variables.

To keep the math simple, the formula used will be at the country level. Worker productivity is the GDP divided by the number of workers (full and part-time). In 1970, the U.S. GDP was $1.1 trillion and there were 102 million workers, so each worker produced an average of $11,000 in goods or services. In "2012 dollars," that is $65,000 per worker. In 2012, the U.S. GDP was $16 trillion and there were 143 million workers, so each worker produced an average of $112,000 in goods or services.

In essence, worker productivity has grown at least 60 percent faster than inflation, yet workers' wages have barely kept up with inflation. This means that workers are producing more money for businesses, but the workers aren't seeing the benefits of their labor. This is one major reason why the rich are getting richer and the financial statuses of the rest of the people in the country are not improving.

Here are some more trends that highlight how Democrats and Republicans have failed Americans:

- In 1920, the wealthiest one percent had 18 percent of the wealth. In 2010, the wealthiest one percent had 35 percent of the wealth. If you eliminate housing, in 2010 the top one percent had 43 percent of the wealth.

- Between 1920 and 1980, working and middle class wages rose at the same rate as worker productivity. After 1980, worker wages barely kept up with inflation while worker productivity soared.

- In 1962, the average minimum wage was $1.15. In 2012, it was $7.25. If the minimum wage from 1962 increased at the rate of inflation, the minimum wage in 2012 would be over $9. If the minimum wage had increased at the same rate as worker productivity, the minimum wage in 2012 would be over $14 an hour.

Stop and think about this for a moment. Imagine a society where the minimum wage rates had kept up with worker productivity. Many people would not require government welfare programs, would not be dependent upon the government, would have enough money to meet essential needs, would have money to cover unexpected costs, would have disposable income, would be self-reliant, and would be happy. Democrats and Republicans have truly failed the American people and killed the American dream.

- In "2003 dollars," the median income in 1970 was $38,000. In "2003 dollars," the median income in 2012 was $42,000. Median income has been nearly stagnant for 40 years, when adjusted for inflation.

- In "2003 dollars," the top three percent of wage earners in 1970 made $95,000 a year. In "2003 dollars," the top three percent in 2012 made over $160,000 a year. The executive class wages have skyrocketed over the last 40 years.

- In 1970, the average CEO made 20 times the income of the average worker. In 2012, the average CEO made 230 times the income of the average worker. CEO pay has skyrocketed, while worker pay has suffered. CEOs are not that much more intelligent than they were 40 years ago. But if CEOs were intelligent, compassionate, and forward thinking, they would find ways to increase all workers' pay, not just their own.

- In 1970, middle income earners took home 63 percent of the total income. In 2010, middle income earners took home less than 45 percent of the total income. If middle income earners still took home 63 percent of the total income, the average middle income wage would be over $80,000 a year.

Adam Smith mentions this in his book *The Wealth of Nations*.

"No society can surely be flourishing and happy, of which the greater part of the members are poor and miserable. It is but equity, besides, that they who feed, cloath and lodge the whole body of the people, should have such a share of the produce of their own labour as to be themselves tolerably well fed, cloathed and lodged.

"All for ourselves, and nothing for other people, seems, in every age of the world, to have been the vile maxim of the masters of mankind.

"What improves the circumstances of the greater part can never be regarded as an inconveniency to the whole. No society can surely be flourishing and happy, of which the far greater part of the members are poor and miserable."

Democrats and Republicans have been doing the same things over and over again for the last 40 years, and the poor, the working poor, the working class, and the mid-middle class keep getting screwed. Independents understand this and want the insanity stopped.

Below are some solutions to help increase the incomes of most Americans:

Learn from other countries like Germany and institute a Co-Determination law, which has many facets and works in conjunction with other laws. Here are the main points of the law.

- All public companies with 1000 or more employees have at least 33 percent of the board of directors consisting of employees.
- All public companies with 2000 or more employees have at least 50 percent of the board of directors consisting of employees.
- Employees are voted onto the board by the other employees.

The benefits of this solution are:

- The employees now have a say in the runnings of the business.
- Government isn't mandating a wage; they are allowing the corporation to function within a regulated marketplace.

- The employees help ensure that the profits and gains in worker productivity are not all given to the executives.
- There are increased wages for all employees of the company.
- There are increased wages for all employees of other companies. Other companies will have to pay higher wages, otherwise they will lose their employees to the larger companies.

Create a Worker Productivity Income law that has similar features to the 401k retirement program. The average pay increases for all employees must be the same percentage as the average pay increase for the top one percent of the highest earners in the company.

Bonuses and Benefits

- Bonuses, benefits, and stock options must be applied equally for all full-time employees.
- CEO compensation (wages, bonuses, stock options, and benefits) cannot exceed 50 times the average employee's compensation and applies to all companies under the parent company's umbrella.

The benefits of this solution are:

- Employees and executives are treated the same.
- CEOs can no longer be treated differently than any other employee.

Two Tiered Minimum Wage

- The first tier is for people less than 25 years old.
- The second tier is for anyone 25 years old or older.
- There are already laws that don't allow companies to discriminate based upon age. These laws can be enhanced to ensure that companies don't discriminate as employees turn 25.

The benefits of this solution are:

- The first tier encourages businesses to hire younger workers who don't have many job skills. This also helps younger workers develop job skills.
- The second tier is for everyone else, and it needs to allow a single income earner to earn at least enough money so that if they are the sole wage earner in a family of four, the family of four lives above the poverty line.

Progressive Minimum Wage (another minimum wage solution)

- Each year, an employee must receive a $1 pay raise until they attain a living wage.

Publicly traded companies must post the following on their web-sites:

- CEO total compensation (pay, bonuses, and benefits).
- Average total compensation for the top 10 percent of earners.
- Average compensation for all American workers and foreign workers.
- Average compensation for the bottom 10 percent of American workers and foreign workers.
- Number of workers and average compensation broken down by country.

    This information is available publicly now, but is not easy to find. As stated previously, making information easily available to the consumer makes it so that the consumer can make informed buying choices, and gives the consumer power.

Create tax incentives to companies for all workers that are full-time and make a living wage of $15 an hour. Or, take the opposite approach and create tax penalties to companies for every full-time worker who makes less than $15 an hour. Tax incentives are preferred, as it is a positive encouragement as opposed to a punishment.

Create tax incentives to companies that provide the same benefits to their part-time workers that they provide to their full-time workers. These include: medical insurance, sick time, vacation time, and bonuses.

15 Taxes

Taxes are the primary source of income for governments. Each layer of government at the local, county, state, or country tier needs taxes to function and provide the services they provide.

The tax system in the United States is extremely complex.
The income tax system has over 500 forms. In 1970, the country's tax rules registry was 19,000 pages long. In 2012, the tax rules registry was over 73,000 pages long.

There are many ways people pay taxes, but there are four primary ways. The first is on income, which is based on wages and bonuses. The second is on the appreciation of wealth. The third is on sales, which is based on what a person purchases. The fourth is on ownership; this is based on owning something, including real estate and automobiles.

Income type taxes are broken down into three subcategories: Income tax, Social Security tax, and Medicare tax. Income tax is taxed based on an adjusted gross income (AGI). It is paid by individuals and by businesses. Individuals can reduce their taxes by having children, paying state income or property taxes, mortgage interest, making charitable contributions, and many other types of deductions.

Businesses can lower their tax burden by documenting the costs of doing business. These include research and development, travel expenses, entertainment expenses, purchases of equipment, purchasing buildings, and showing losses on investments.

Please note: The tax rates discussed are for 2012. The tax rates, rules, deductions, and loopholes are always changing.

Personal income taxes are progressive and based upon the filing status. There are many tax deductions individuals can take to lower their incomes and reduce their tax rates. To give an example of the progressive nature of the tax, here are the income tax rates, rounded to the nearest thousandth, for a married couple filing jointly:

- 10 percent up to $17,000
- 15 percent between $17,000 and $71,000
- 25 percent between $71,000 and $143,000
- 28 percent between $143,000 and $217,000
- 33 percent between $217,000 and $388,000
- 35 percent on anything over $388,000

Social Security tax requires the employer pay a 6.2 percent tax for each employee and the employee to also pay a 6.2 percent tax. This creates a 12.4 percent total tax that goes into Social Security. However, this tax is not required once an employee's wages are over a certain amount, which changes each year. In 2012, the employer and the employee paid Social Security on wages up to $110,000. Once an employee made more than $110,000, no more Social Security taxes had to be paid by the employer or the employee.

Medicare is taxed at 1.45 percent of all wages and bonuses. This tax is paid by both the employee and the employer. There is no cap income for Medicare taxes. Medicare taxes are not paid on capital gains.

Businesses have a different income tax system. Businesses are taxed based on their profits, not on total sales. There are many tax deductions businesses can take to lower their profits. The corporate tax rates are rounded and are as follows:

- 15 percent up to $50,000
- 25 percent between $50,000 and $75,000
- 34 percent between $75,000 and $100,000
- 39 percent between $100,000 and $335,000
- 34 percent between $335,000 and $10 million
- 35 percent between $10 million and $15 million
- 38 percent between $15 million and $18 million
- 35 percent on anything over $18 million

The appreciation of wealth is taxed based on long term capital gains. Capital gain is wealth generated from an increase in the value of an asset, when the asset is sold. If the value of stock increases and the stock is sold, that is capital gain. If capital gains are kept for less than a year, then they are taxed as income. In 2012, if the capital gains were long-term (kept for more than a year), then they were taxed at a flat 15 percent. The reason for the lower long-term capital gains tax rate is to encourage investors to keep money invested and help stabilize the economy.

The way capital gains are taxed opens up a loophole that many investors take advantage of. If the stock they purchased is losing money, they will sell it within a year of purchasing it. This reduces their tax rate at the income tax rate. If the stock is making money and they hold it for more than one year, when they sell the stock they only have to pay a capital gains tax rate.

Sales taxes are a flat rate. They are based on what type of purchase is being made. The federal government only has sales tax on items such as gasoline and alcohol. Many states and local tax authorities have taxes on all purchases including food, clothes, gasoline, alcohol, cars, etc.

Ownership tax is based on owning something. For automobiles, the tax includes state stickers and other types of taxes. Ownership tax on real estate is known as property taxes, which is based on the property value of the real estate. If the property tax rate is 2.5 percent, then a person who owns a $100,000 house would pay $2,500 annually in property tax. The problem with this tax is that the person may owe $90,000 to the bank and actually only owns ten percent, or $10,000, of the property value; yet they have to pay taxes based upon the total property value of $100,000. If all wealth was taxed the same way as property is, then people would not be taxed on the appreciation of wealth, but on their entire wealth.

To illustrate how tax burdens impact families, let's compare a middle class family's income tax burden to an executive class family's income tax burden. This is just a single variation designed to point out some of the issues with the tax structure. It doesn't include any tax deductions, even the non-itemized standard deductions; it will be based solely upon income. The deductions distort the picture of what the tax rate is, and the deductions usually benefit the executive class more than they benefit the middle class.

Assume the middle class family has no children, makes $75,000 a year in wages and bonuses, doesn't have any income tax deductions, and doesn't have any stocks or investment properties.

The family would pay an income tax of $10,800.

> 10 percent of $17,000 = $1,700
> 15 percent of $54,000 = $8,100
> 25 percent of $4,000 = $1,000

The family would pay Social Security taxes of $4,650.

The family would pay Medicare taxes of $1,090.

The total taxes paid by the middle income class family would be $16,510, or roughly 22 percent of their income.

Assume an executive class family that has no children, makes $225,000 a year in wages and bonuses, doesn't have any income tax deductions and made $75,000 a year in capital gains for a total income of $300,000 (or four times the amount of money the middle income tax family made).

The family would pay an income tax of: $51,160.

> 10 percent of $17,000 = $1,700
> 15 percent of $54,000 = $8,100
> 25 percent of $72,000 = $18,000
> 28 percent of $74,000 = $20,720
> 33 percent of $8,000 = $2,640

The family would pay Social Security taxes of $7,000.

The family would pay Medicare taxes of $3,265.

The family would pay capital gains taxes of $11,250.

The total taxes paid by the executive class family would be $72,765, or roughly 24 percent of their income.

If the executive class family made all their income from investments, they would pay $56,250 in taxes, or 15 percent of their income.

The take-home pay for the middle income family would be $58,490. If the cost of living were $50,000 a year, then the middle income family would have $8,490 in disposable income. This leaves very little money for emergencies, college, retirement savings, replacing a car, or a vacation.

The take-home pay for the executive class family would be $227,235. If their cost of living were three times that of the middle income family at $150,000, the executive class family would still have $77,235 in disposable income. Only a fraction of that would go toward retirement savings; the remainder could be spent on emergencies, vacations, and putting money into even more investments.

Democrats are always pushing for more tax increases on the rich and stating how they need to make the tax system more fair. Democrats believe paying taxes is a civic responsibility. Taxes are needed for infrastructure, safety nets, environmental protection and all the other government activities that benefit society and help keep it safe.

The problem with the Democrats and their beliefs isn't that they want to make the tax system more fair; it's that the taxes never fix the country's problems. All the changes to the tax system are irrelevant if government spending isn't brought under control. Democrats keep increasing taxes and keep increasing government spending. If government spending isn't controlled, then Democrats will always have to keep increasing taxes. This isn't fair to any taxpayer.

Republicans believe that cutting taxes is what is best for the country. Republicans believe that cutting taxes increases the money available to be invested into businesses, which helps the businesses and the economy grow and thrive.

Republicans also believe that an increase to the capital gains tax will hurt the economy. Republicans believe that investors won't invest money into stocks and businesses if the capital gains tax were to increase. In the last 30 years, the capital gains tax rate has fallen from 28 percent to 15 percent.

The first problem with Republicans' beliefs is that a growing economy has not increased wages for 95 percent of Americans. As was stated earlier, the trends of the last 40 years show the average American's wages have only increased by the rate of inflation.

Another problem with Republicans' beliefs is that they believe investors won't buy stocks and invest in businesses if the capital gains tax is too high. Small business owners' incomes are taxed at the income tax rate, which is as high as 35 percent. Small business owners still invest in their businesses, even with these high tax rates. If small business owners would invest in their business at a 35 percent tax rate, then so would investors. If the capital gains tax rate were the same as the income tax rate, investors would still buy stocks and invest in businesses.

The current tax structure concepts try to be fair, but the concepts are not the actual tax structure. It seems fair that incomes are taxed based upon a progressive system. It seems fair that wealth building (capital gains) are taxed at a different rate than incomes. It seems fair that sales taxes are flat rates and based upon purchases.

A relevant quote from Adam Smith's book *The Wealth of Nations*:

"The subjects of every state ought to contribute towards the support of the government, as nearly as possible, in proportion to their respective abilities; that is, in proportion to the revenue which they respectively enjoy under the protection of the state."

The concepts seem fair; it's how the structure is implemented that isn't fair. The tax structure is way too complicated. In 2007, almost 60 percent of individual income taxes were filed by paid preparers. If most individuals can't fill out their own tax forms, the system is too complicated. The progressive income tax system isn't truly progressive. There are many loopholes and deductions that the executive class can take that aren't available to most Americans.

One example of how unfair the tax structure is relates to capital gains. That capital gains taxes are at 15 percent to encourage wealth building is fine. However, once a person's income from capital gains reaches a certain point, that capital gain is now income and should be taxed as such. Many people in the executive class make more money from capital gains than they do from wages and bonuses.

Another example of the poor tax structure is tax havens. Tax havens are usually in countries that charge little or no tax. Individuals or companies setup shell companies in these countries and find ways to push sales and capital expenditures through these shell companies with the intent of avoiding paying taxes in America.

In 2012, the Tax Justice Network issued a report that untaxed wealth in offshore tax havens was between $21 to $32 trillion. The TJN estimates that over half the world's trade passes through tax havens.

Taxes are required for any country to maintain its infrastructure, protect its citizens, and keep the country whole. Many individuals and companies who claim they are not breaking any tax laws may be accurate. However, the tax laws are being created by the government working in conjunction with wealthy individuals and large companies to their mutual benefit. People who are not in the executive class have to pay for the loopholes and tax havens that the executive class and large corporations enjoy.

Fixing the tax structure requires crossing into other aspects of governance. The tax structure can't allow the government to keep increasing spending. The tax structure must ensure that incomes for 95 percent of Americans increase at the same rate as the executive class incomes. It must encourage economic growth of businesses, encourage wealth and retirement savings, encourage American job creation, and ensure that individuals and corporations are paying what society considers to be a fair share.

Below are some solutions to help bring about a tax structure that benefits the country as a whole:

Create tax incentives for businesses to increase the number of American workers and increase the pay/benefits to workers.

Create tax penalties for businesses if they outsource jobs to other countries, lay people off, or don't provide part-time workers equal benefits.

Make it illegal for Congresspeople or anybody on their staff to use outside services to complete their income taxes. They must fill out their own taxes. The benefit of this is that it will force Congress to simplify the personal income tax law.

Create a Tax Review Jury

- Make the Voters Jury responsible for all laws except tax laws. Make the Tax Review Jury responsible for all tax laws. They have the same authority and responsibility as the Voters Jury.

Create a Taxes Information Superhighway that shows the following:

- All income and taxes paid by all politicians and their staffs.
- All income and taxes paid by all political lobbyists.
- All income and taxes paid by all public corporations.

Visit websites such as Citizens for Tax Justice (www.CTJ.org), the Tax Justice Network USA(www.tjn-usa.org), and the Tax Justice Network (www.taxjustice.net). These sites and others are great places to learn other ways to clean up the tax code.

16 Politicians vs. Voters

John Dalberg-Acton once said, "Power tends to corrupt, and absolute power corrupts absolutely."

Politicians talk about how much they want to help people and how much they want to help the country. In 2012, less than 20 percent of the voters approved of the job the U.S. Congress was doing, yet incumbents have a reelection rate above 90 percent. Congressional approval ratings are not important to politicians because the ratings are based upon Congress as a whole. Surveys show that voters within a district or a state give their representatives a greater than 50 percent rating. The voters tend to believe their senator or representative isn't the problem; it's all the other Congresspeople from all the other states who are the problem.

Voters have jobs, families, and lives. They don't have time to pay much attention to what politicians promise or what politicians actually do. This is why people usually vote along political party lines. Voters support their party because of their party's brand. The brand their party espouses is in line with their voters' beliefs. Most voters don't even know who their representatives are. The voters are content as long as their representatives are from their political party.

The three-cup con game is a game where the con man has a ball hidden under one of three cups. The con shows the customer the ball under one of the cups, then moves the cups around. The customer places a bet and tries to pick which cup has the ball. The customer placing the bet has no chance; the con man is an illusionist and controls the game. The con man only lets you win when he wants you to win. He does this to keep you playing.

The reason Congress has an abysmal approval rating, yet voters believe their local politicians are doing an adequate job, is best explained with the three-cup con game analogy. Politicians keep their power because they create the illusion that they care about the voters; voters are allowed to see the ball that is under one of the cups. What is under the one cup is all the voters expect to see; they don't realize that the politicians are playing the three-cup con game and the voters are being conned.

Democratic voters expect their politicians to protect the environment and act as a counterbalance to the greed of businesses.

Solyndra was a solar panel manufacturing company based in California. In early 2009, the Bush administration (Republican) turned down giving a government-backed loan to Solyndra because the government said the company wasn't economically viable. Later in 2009, the Obama administration (Democrat) gave Solyndra a loan of over $500 million. In 2011, Solyndra filed for bankruptcy (the Republicans were right; it's a shock, but it can happen), and the taxpayers lost $500 million that will never be recovered. The ball under the cup the voters saw was that the Democrats wanted to help an environmentally friendly company and were trying to protect the environment.

Under the second cup was the first con. The con was that the company was not economically viable. The executives of the business were not capable of actually building the business. The executives only cared about getting as much money from the government as they could.

Under the third cup was the other con. In 2009, Solyndra executives donated hundreds of thousands of dollars to the Obama campaign. The government was not trying to protect the environment, and they weren't trying to act as a counterbalance to the greed in businesses. The Democratic politicians were bought by the business.

Democratic voters expect their politicians to be caring and compassionate. The voters expect politicians to help the poor. The voters expect politicians to support higher wages. The voters expect politicians to continue supporting food stamps, Social Security, Medicare, Medicaid and all the other welfare programs that many voters need in order to survive.

Democratic politicians keep showing the voters the ball that is under cup one by always saying how they support higher wages and that they support the welfare programs.

What is under cup two is the first con. If Democratic politicians actually cared about the voters and the lower income and middle income class, they would create programs that built in long-term increases to the wages and incomes of these classes. There would be a living wage. The Democrats would build a strong wealth and retirement program. The con is that Democrats are not caring and compassionate. The con is that the Democratic politicians are keeping the wages low and keeping people poor so that the people stay dependent upon the government and keep voting Democrats into office.

Under the third cup is another part of the con. The politicians hold fundraisers where patrons pay $40,000 for a dinner. If voters donated $40 to a politician's campaign, it would take 1000 voters to donate the amount of money a single rich person does. Who do you believe the Democrat politician is going to listen to? The single person who donated $40,000, or the 1000 people (whom they've never met) who donated $40? The con is that the Democratic politicians listen to the rich (whom they met at their fundraisers), and not the voters.

Republican voters expect their politicians to work for businesses and to support a competitive marketplace.

Under the first cup, Republican voters see the politicians constantly fighting to deregulate. Decreasing the number of government regulations is supposed to help create a competitive marketplace that helps businesses grow.

Under the second cup is the first con. The Republicans create laws that favor big businesses. An example of this is the new patent law. For hundreds of years, the law was "first to invent," but in 2011 it was changed to "first to file." This forces the small inventor to file patents immediately instead of working on and perfecting the invention before filing. After the small inventor got the product working, they could file updated or offshoot patents. The new law is a huge advantage to large corporations who can see what patents have been filed and then have their engineers look at all the possible offshoot technologies. The big business then preemptively files patents on all the possible offshoot technologies and blocks the small inventor from owning those offshoot patents.

Under the third cup is another con. The con is the tax structure. Small business owners have to pay income tax on all profits. Smaller businesses with smaller profits have a tax rate as high as 39 percent, whereas businesses with profits higher than $18 million have a tax rate of 35 percent.

Under the fourth cup (they are con men, they can have as many cups and cons as they like) is another part of the con. Republican voters support the concept of fewer government regulations and creating a competitive marketplace. However, the con is what regulations are removed and what regulations are kept in place.

Republican politicians have deregulated the industry to make buying up smaller companies easier. Republican politicians claim they are deregulating and keeping the voters happy, but they are actually deregulating to keep big business happy. By making laws that allow big businesses to buy out small businesses, there is less competition in the marketplace. Large businesses have the financial resources to donate to Republican politicians, and in reciprocation Republican politicians make laws that allow the big businesses to buy up the competition.

Republican voters expect their politicians to fight for a smaller government against the socialist Democrats.

Under the first cup, Republican voters see the Republican politicians talking about reducing budgets and keeping government spending small. Republican politicians keep voters scared of the big socialist Democrats and the big government the Democrats support. Republican politicians tell voters that they are the only politicians who will protect the voters from a big government.

Under the second cup is the first con. Republicans have only fought for smaller government and less spending when a Democrat was President. When it was a Republican President, the government budget increased at a much faster rate. There are many examples of this, none more so than George Bush's presidency of 2001 to 2009. In 2001, the U.S. budget was $1.86 trillion. In 2009, it was $3.52 trillion. That is an annual increase of eight percent.

Under the third cup is another part of the con. Republican politicians tell voters how Socialism does nothing but make people dependent on the government and that it intrudes on people's lives and takes away their money and freedoms.

The Medicare Prescription Drug program was overhauled by Republicans in 2003. The Republican politicians told voters that the program would only cost $40 billion a year and would help 25 million senior citizens pay for their drug prescriptions. That is a cost of $1600 per senior citizen.

In 2010, the program cost $60 billion to administer and approximately 27 million people used the program. That is a cost of $2222 per senior citizen, or an increase of almost 40 percent.

The above figures don't sound too bad, until you really look under the third cup and see the real con. The law is loved by the pharmaceutical companies that provide prescription drugs because there were no cost containment rules. Republican politicians made it illegal for the government to negotiate drug prices with the drug companies. The law says drug companies can charge the government the marketplace prices. The Republican politicians are not fighting against Socialism and bigger government; they are purposefully creating a larger government by not allowing the largest customer (the government) to negotiate prices.

Independents realize that it's not just each political party pulling the con game against their voters; both the Democratic and Republican parties also work together to keep the cons going.

Insider stock trading is illegal for the voters. It wasn't illegal for politicians or their staff. As the voters finally saw this injustice, they demanded the politicians do something to fix the problem.

In April 2012, Congress passed the Stock Act, which made insider trading illegal for politicians and their staff.

In April 2013, the Democratic and Republican politicians decided to pull another con on the voters. The politicians repealed part of the Stock Act, and congressional staff members no longer had to report their financial transactions. The politicians made it okay for their staff members to do insider stock trading because there wouldn't be any proof that staff members had done any.

Another con is the unemployment rate. To voters, the unemployment rate is the percentage of the population looking for a job. In January 2012, the government reported the unemployment rate as 8.3 percent. The con that is pulled on the voters is that the rate does not count the number of part-time workers who want a full-time job. The rate does not count the number of people who got so frustrated that they quit looking for a job. The rate does not count the people who were desperate and took any job they could find, jobs that are way below their skill level. If the above rules were factored into the unemployment rate, the rate would have been 15 percent.

The Senate has a code of ethics and its own ethics review committee. The House of Representatives has a code of ethics and its own ethics review committee. Considering how both houses allow insider trading for their staff members and report a misleading unemployment rate, their ethics are questionable. Considering how both houses ethics review committees are made up of their fellow Congresspeople, the inquiries of the ethics review committees are questionable.

Independents are frustrated with the Democratic and Republican politicians who keep playing the con game. Independents are disappointed with the Democratic and Republican voters because the voters keep their eyes closed and keep allowing themselves to be conned.

The Democratic and Republican politicians claim that if there really were a problem, the voters would vote out the politicians. But the fact remains, this isn't happening. The politicians are taking and keeping power, and the corruption that comes with holding power is hurting the country.

Here are some solutions to help reduce the power of politicians and start to give power back to the citizens:

Congresspeople can only serve for a total of 12 years in Congress, total. They cannot serve 12 years in the Senate, and then switch to the House of Representatives. This law would limit how much power politicians could gain by not allowing them to build power over decades.

Congress must abide by ALL laws it creates and cannot exempt themselves or their staff members.

Politicians and government workers are not allowed to be lobbyists.

Politicians and government workers can't receive pensions from multiple government agencies. They are only allowed one pension.

Create the following laws and make the information available on an Open Government Information Superhighway:

- All government workers and politicians must post which lobbyists they meet with.
- All donations to politicians, political parties, and any political group (PAC, Super PAC, and others) must be posted. Individual donations must include the donor's name and nationality. Donations by organizations must include all board members' names and nationalities.
- All lobbyists must post their names and nationality, money spent on lobbying, and dates and times of who was lobbied.

Create an Ethics Jury

- Create a code of ethics that all politicians, staff members, lobbyists, and all government employees must abide by.
- Any violations are reviewed by the jury, not by fellow politicians.

17 Grassroots Solutions

In 2009, a grassroots movement known as the Tea Party was formed to protest large and inefficient government. The Tea Party members were tired of the government being fiscally irresponsible and only wanting to keep increasing its size. Most of the members of the Tea Party were Republicans.

In 2011, a grassroots movement known as Occupy Wall Street (OWS) was formed to protest large businesses and their greedy executives. The OWS members were tired of Wall Street and other members of the executive class who were financially greedy and only wanting to increase how much money they could make. Most of the members of OWS were Democrats.

The two movements were protesting the rich and powerful. The two movements should have realized that they shared a common theme and should have started working together to form a powerful and self-sustaining grassroots movement. But as is typical with Democrats and Republicans, the two movements started bickering with each other and saw the other movement as flawed. Each movement only saw itself as the correct movement and believed the people in the other movement were nothing but a bunch of uninformed idiots.

It is this bickering that the government class and the executive class want. They want the voters and the citizens fighting amongst themselves so that they can keep the power and wealth that they have accumulated over the years.

The rules need to be changed. The rules need to stop favoring the rich, powerful, wealthy, and connected. The rules need to start favoring the majority of the government's customers.

The only way new rules will be enacted is with a grassroots movement. It was grassroots movements that gave women the right to vote, that gave minorities in the country equal rights, and that made it so that businesses couldn't exploit children as workers.

As you have read the book, you can see that there are many ways to fix problems within the country. The news media and government officials are wrong when they say how complex the problems are and that we have many challenges in resolving the problems. The problems and solutions are NOT complex. If a systematic and logical approach to fixing problems is implemented, the problems can be resolved and solutions that work for everyone can be implemented.

"To widen the market and to narrow the competition, is always the interest of the dealers … The proposal of any new law or regulation of commerce which comes from this order, ought always to be listened to with great precaution, and ought never to be adopted till after having been long and carefully examined, not only with the most scrupulous, but with the most suspicious attention. It comes from an order of men, whose interest is never exactly the same with that of the public, who have generally an interest to deceive and even oppress the public, and who accordingly have, upon many occasions, both deceived and oppressed it."
--Adam Smith, *The Wealth of Nations*

Many politicians have stated that they only pay attention to a cause if they receive enough emails and phone calls calling for action. That means the people have to be involved, the people have to contact their representative on a weekly basis.

Congress has a 20 percent approval rating; that means 80 percent of the people are frustrated with Congress. Are you one of those people? Are you frustrated? Do you believe there has to be a better way? Then do something about it. Don't wait for someone else to do something. *You* have to do something.

Many movements call for members to contact their representative. This is just silly because most people don't even know who their representative is, so the movements die right then and there.

As an IT person, I know it's critical to make things as easy as possible. If step-by-step guidance is provided, the steps are easy to follow, and most importantly the solution makes sense, then most people willingly climb on board. They will become active members of the movement.

There is an old saying: "A boss gets people to do what he wants, a leader gets people to want what he wants." Most failed movements try to tell people to change; hopefully, with this book, you *want* change. You *want* to get involved. You *want* to make things better. And you believe that you can.

Step 1:
Visit the website www.solutionalpolitics.com.

All the solutions in the book exist on the website and at the end of this chapter.

Step 2:
On the website is a link to other websites where you can find out who your representative is, who your senators are, and how to contact them.

To find your representative:
http://www.house.gov/representatives/find/

To find your senator:
http://www.senate.gov/

Note: Many senators don't provide their email address but provide a contact form on their website.

Step 3:
Start an email to your representative, senator, or both.

Copy and paste any solutions from www.solutionalpolitics.com that you want to include in the email.

Make changes to the solutions if you want.

Step 4:
Send the email.

Step 5:
Tell all your friends and families to read the book so they can build a foundation of knowledge and understanding. Tell them of the problems with the country and what solutions could fix the problems. Discuss the book and see what other solutions people think of. Keep building the grassroots movement.

Step 6:
Rinse and repeat steps 1 through 5 every week until you are satisfied the country is moving in the right direction.

This is **how one person (you) CAN make a difference**. Don't fail yourself.

Below are the solutions from the book, reorganized and regrouped.

Information Superhighways

The concept is to make information easy to find and readily available, which subsequently gives power back to the people. Google transformed how people search the Internet, Facebook transformed how people socially interact on the Internet, the information superhighways objective will transform how people can promote the general welfare.

The government information superhighway contains:

- All departments are included, with a hierarchy from the top down.
- Information is available by the common use name and the department's name. Example: food stamps is the common use name; SNAP is the government name.
- Results of government fiscal audits.
- Government budgets, the justifications for the budgets, and actual spending.
- Administration costs and the administration cost percentages in comparison to the budgets and actual costs.

- Number of people receiving benefits and average benefits received.
- List the SMART objectives and how well the department performed against the objectives.
- List the measurements of success and how well the department performed against the metrics. Example: all veterans benefit requests will be processed within 10 working days.
- All government workers' and politicians' meetings and with whom they met.
- All donations to politicians, political parties, and any political group (PAC, Super PAC, and others). All donations must include the donor's name and nationality. Donations by organizations must include all board members' names and nationalities.
- All lobbyists' names and nationalities, money spent on lobbying, and dates and times of who was lobbied.

Government laws and regulations information superhighway:

- All laws and regulations with easy search and navigation.
- What laws have passed the SMART objectives review.
- What laws are currently under SMART objective review and the laws' status.
- What the Six Sigma agencies findings have been and what they are working on.
- What regulations are under review by the Regulations Jury.

Taxes information superhighway:

- All income and taxes paid by all politicians and their staffs.
- All income and taxes paid by all political lobbyists.
- All income and taxes paid by all public corporations.
- All income and taxes paid by the top one percent in wages and wealth.

Healthcare information superhighway:

- Each medical facility is required to report the following information to the above agency and post it on their website: income, expenses, core minor and major medical procedures performed, price of each different type of procedure, price of each medicine, average patient hospital time for each procedure, mortality rates, success rates, and a patient satisfaction survey.
- All insurance companies must report the following information to the above agency and post it on their website: income, expenses, top 10 highest paid executives' salaries, procedures covered, procedures not covered, price of each different procedure covered, and the price of each medicine covered.

Juries

The concept is to provide voters with information and a voice in the legislative process. It gives power back to the American people.

Voters Jury
Reviews all laws before and sometimes after they are signed.

- This jury consists of 12 of people who would be affected by the law.
- This jury has recommendation powers only; they can't change the laws.
- The jury has 90 days to review a law.
- No law can be signed prior to jury review, unless there is a two-thirds congressional approval of the law (this covers emergency situations).
- All funds for a law must exist in the law. Funds that are not part of the intent of the law must be added as an addendum and clearly identified.
- Ensure that the laws are designed with the objective of a framework that allows businesses the best potential of growing and succeeding within capitalism, while protecting society.
- Ensure that the law does not benefit one company, marketplace, government agency, government worker, or lobbyist.

- Ensure that the law does not exempt one company, marketplace, government agency, government worker, or lobbyist.
- Ensure that the law is meeting its SMART objectives. If it isn't, the voters jury can nullify the law.

Ethics Jury

Create a code of ethics that all politicians, staff members, lobbyists, and all government employees must abide by.

- Any violations are reviewed by the jury, not by fellow politicians.

Tax Review Jury

Make the Voters Jury responsible for all laws except tax laws. Make the Tax Review Jury responsible for all tax laws. They have the same authority and responsibility as the Voters Jury.

Regulations Jury

Reviews all regulations before they go into effect or all queries from people trying to understand the regulations.

- This jury would be 12 people; four people who would directly benefit from the law, four people who would be directly and negatively affected by the law, and four people who would not be affected by the law.
- It only takes nine members of the jury to approve regulations.
- The jury can stop the regulations from going into effect and can force the regulations to be rewritten.
- A person who is directly impacted by a regulation can ask for clarification of a regulation by the regulations jury.
- The person asking for clarification cannot be a lawyer, associated with a law firm, or a lobbyist. The person must clearly explain how they were negatively affected by the regulations. The person cannot have a net worth of more than $1 million.
- The regulations jury can cancel all fines, lawsuits, and grievances against the person asking for clarification.

Accounting, budgets, and fiscal responsibility
The concept is to ensure the government has accurate accounting, realistic budgets, is efficiently run, and is fiscally responsible.

Each governmental department's budget is frozen until the department can pass a GAO audit.

Create multiple non-profit organizations that perform audits on the government. Each non-profit would specialize in an area of the government. The results of the GAO audits and the non-profit organizations audits must be published side by side so there are checks and balances on both audits.

Justification of each budget. The government must document at a detailed and summary level the justification for any changes in the budget. The justifications must show solid, relevant, and factual information proving the program's effectiveness and worth. The justifications must show the measurements of success and how well the programs performed against the metrics. The justification must show historical trends and projected trends.

Congress and the President cannot increase their pay unless the budget is balanced for the year.

Total federal government spending cannot increase above inflation, without voter approval or a two-thirds majority vote by Congress. This allows department budgets to increase faster than inflation if required, but not the entire federal government spending.

General Concepts
The concept is to help bring stability and standards to the government and economic policy.

On a fundamental level, utilize supply side economics if trying to drive the economy toward a more society-friendly goal, like green energy, new technologies, or conservation. Utilize supply side economics to manage inflation and help keep the economy on an even keel. Utilize demand side economics as the foundation to the economy. Use it to increase wages and benefit the people.

Study countries like Canada and Germany. Their economies are based on capitalism, but the government provides social guidance and economic corrections. See how these philosophies can be applied in America.

Learn from other countries like Germany and institute a Co-Determination law.

- All public companies with 1000 or more employees must have at least 33 percent of the board of directors consisting of employees.
- All public companies with 2000 or more employees must have at least 50 percent of the board of directors consisting of employees.
- Employees are voted onto the board by the other employees.

Publicly traded companies must post the following on their websites:

- CEO total compensation (pay, bonuses, and benefits).
- Average total compensation for the top 10 percent of earners.
- Average compensation for all American workers and foreign workers.
- Average compensation for the bottom 10 percent of American workers and foreign workers.
- Number of workers and average compensation broken down by country.

Create laws that make business executives of publicly traded companies financially accountable for business failures (just like small business owners are). If a business files for bankruptcy, some laws could include:

- Executives are not allowed any bonuses or pay raises while the company is in bankruptcy.

- All bonuses and stock options paid to the executives from the previous two years must be paid back to the company.
- The executives must continue working for the company until it climbs out of bankruptcy, unless they are fired. If they are fired, they are not allowed any bonuses or any forms of extra compensation (i.e. golden parachutes).

A company cannot purchase another company if the acquisition makes the company one of the five largest companies in the market sector. Limit the number of acquisitions any company can make to two a year. Strengthen the Sherman Act (which doesn't allow monopolies) and the Clayton and Federal Trade Commission Act (which prohibits monopolistic mergers and anti-competitive mergers).

Government must maintain a five percent reserve of the budget, and it must function within a balanced budget. If the economy is in trouble, the government can tap into the five percent reserve and inject money into the economy. By having a five percent reserve, the government doesn't have to borrow money when the economy needs help. Once the economy has recovered, the government goes back to building up the five percent reserve.

All healthcare facilities are encouraged to become non-profit organizations. Health insurance companies are encouraged to become either non-profit organizations or cooperatives. Government incentives and rewards should be provided for the most efficient and effective healthcare facilities and insurance companies.

Taxes, incentives and penalties
The concept is to encourage the government and businesses to work towards a better society.

Make it illegal for Congresspeople or anybody on their staff to use outside services to complete their income taxes. They must fill out their own taxes.

Create tax incentives for businesses to increase the number of American workers and increase the pay/benefits to workers. Create tax penalties for jobs that are moved overseas.

Create tax incentives to companies for all workers that are full-time and make a living wage of $15 an hour. Or, take the opposite approach and create tax penalties for companies for every full-time worker who makes less than $15 an hour. Tax incentives are preferred, as it is a positive encouragement as opposed to a punishment.

Create tax incentives to companies that provide the same benefits to their part-time workers that they provide to their full-time workers. These include medical insurance, sick time, vacation time, and bonuses.

Create tax incentives for investment management firms to help smaller investors who have as little as $10,000 in savings. These firms receive the incentives if they make most of their money based upon how much money the customer makes.

Create tax penalties for businesses if they outsource jobs to other countries, lay people off, or don't provide part-time workers equal benefits.

Income, wealth and retirement
The concept is to increase the income and wealth for most American citizens.

Create a Worker Productivity Income law. The average pay increases for all employees must be the same percentage as the average pay increase for the top one percent of the highest earners in the company.

Bonuses and Benefits

- Bonuses, benefits, and stock options must be applied equally for all full-time employees.
- CEO compensation (wages, bonuses, stock options, and benefits) cannot exceed 50 times the average employee's

compensation and applies to all companies under the parent company's umbrella.

Two Tiered Minimum Wage

- The first tier is for people less than 25 years old.
- The second tier is for anyone 25 years old or older.
- There are already laws that don't allow companies to discriminate based upon age. These laws can be enhanced to ensure that companies don't discriminate as employees turn 25.

Progressive Minimum Wage (another minimum wage solution)

- Each year an employee works for a business they must receive a $1 pay raise until he attains a living wage.

For all businesses that have 20 or more employees, the government must provide 401k plans. They must contribute a minimum of five percent of the employee's pay. Employees making less than $100,000 are required to contribute three percent of their pay. This needs to be done in conjunction with the changes to the Social Security tax. The increase in retirement money the employee is forced to put aside is offset by a decrease in the Social Security tax, making it so that most employees' net income doesn't change.

Social Security tax is changed to three percent on all incomes (wages, bonuses, and capital gains) without a cap. If a person earns $1 million in bonuses or capital gains, they have to pay the three percent into Social Security on that money. The Social Security payouts to the beneficiaries remain the same. This means that extremely high income earners are supplementing Social Security to help it stay a long-term and viable program.

The Social Security trust fund must be untouchable by any other government agency. The government cannot spend the money it gets from Social Security when Social Security buys the special issue securities that it is required to purchase. The government must make sure it sets aside enough money to cover the special issue securities and the interest they accumulate.

The 401k programs must have the option of a guaranteed minimum return of three percent or the rate of inflation, whichever is higher. This makes the program stable and reliable and gives employees a guaranteed amount of money when they retire. Having a minimum isn't hard to implement; many life insurance companies already have a guaranteed minimum rate of return of three percent on life insurance policies. This is done because they can earn higher than a three percent rate of return on their investments but only have to pay out a guaranteed three percent.

Schools must teach the rule of 72 and income and wealth building to all high school students.

On an annual basis, businesses and the government must provide a two-hour session on retirement planning for all employees.

Political Power
The concept is to ensure that politicians don't become too powerful and corrupt.

Congresspeople can only serve for a total of 12 years in the Congress. They cannot serve 12 years in the Senate, and then switch to the House of Representatives. This law would limit how much power politicians could gain by not allowing them to build power over decades.

Members of Congress must abide by ALL laws it creates and cannot exempt themselves or their staff members.

Politicians and government workers are not allowed to be lobbyists.

Politicians and government workers can't receive pensions from multiple government agencies. They are only allowed one pension.

Government Efficiency

The concept is to make the government more efficient and accountable for taxpayer money.

All laws must have one, five and 15-year SMART objectives. The GAO, as a part of its annual audits, determines if the laws are meeting their objectives. If the GAO determines that the law isn't meeting more than 50 percent of the objectives, the government is given one year to rewrite and correct the law. The Voters Jury then reviews the corrections.

Create a government Six Sigma agency that is responsible for cleaning up and modernizing government departments and written regulations. The agency works in conjunction with the GAO for ensuring that laws are meeting their SMART objectives. The agency has a voice in eliminating government departments and regulations that are no longer needed.

About The Author

I grew up near Seattle, Washington, where I spent a lot of time outdoors working on the family farm, hiking, fishing, swimming, and snowmobiling. I moved to Chicago, Illinois, to attend college, met a girl, and fell in love. I now do house chores, mow the lawn, and do stuff with the kids. I've been married for 203 dog years.